Vineyard to Table

The Complete Guide to Wine Production and Enjoyment

Margaret Pierce

loss due to the information herein, either directly or indirectly. Respective authors own all copyrights not held by the publisher. The information herein is offered for informational purposes solely, and is universal as so. The presentation of the information is without contract or any type of guarantee assurance. The trademarks that are used are without any consent, and the publication of the trademark is without permission or backing by the trademark owner. All trademarks and brands within this book are for clarifying purposes only and are the owned by the owners themselves, not affiliated with this document.

Table of Contents

Chapter 1

The History of Wine

Ancient Beginnings

Wine has been an integral part of human culture for thousands of years. The story of wine begins in the cradle of civilization, where ancient peoples discovered the transformative power of fermented grapes. This chapter delves into the early history of wine, tracing its origins, cultural significance, and the evolution of winemaking techniques from prehistoric times through the classical eras of Greece and Rome.

The earliest evidence of wine production dates back to around 6000 BCE in the region that is now Georgia. Archaeologists uncovered pottery fragments with traces of tartaric acid, a key indicator of wine residue. This discovery suggests that early humans were already cultivating grapes and experimenting with fermentation long before recorded history. These ancient vintners likely stumbled upon the process by accident, perhaps noticing that wild grapes left in a container would ferment naturally, producing an intoxicating liquid.

As agriculture developed, so did viticulture. The domestication of the grapevine can be traced to the Near East, particularly in the areas of present-day Iran and Turkey. The ancient Mesopotamians, who inhabited the fertile crescent between the Tigris and Euphrates rivers, played a crucial role in the early history of wine. They not only cultivated grapes but also developed early winemaking techniques. Cuneiform tablets from this period provide detailed accounts of grape harvesting, winemaking, and wine consumption, highlighting its importance in their society.

Wine held a significant place in religious and social rituals. The Sumerians, one of the earliest known civilizations, considered wine a gift from the gods. It was used in religious ceremonies and offered to deities. This practice was not unique to Mesopotamia; similar customs were observed in ancient Egypt, where wine was associated with the god Osiris and played a vital role in funerary rites. Tomb paintings and inscriptions reveal that the Egyptians produced wine and stored it in amphorae, large clay jars that became a standard method of wine storage for millennia.

The spread of viticulture and winemaking to the Mediterranean basin marked a significant expansion in the history of wine. The Phoenicians, renowned seafarers and traders, were instrumental in spreading grape cultivation and winemaking techniques throughout the region. By the first millennium BCE, they had established vineyards in their colonies across North Africa, Spain, and the southern coast of France. Their trade networks ensured that wine became a staple in the diets and cultural practices of many Mediterranean civilizations.

In ancient Greece, wine was deeply woven into the fabric of daily life. It was consumed at symposia, social gatherings where intellectuals and artists discussed philosophy, politics, and literature while enjoying wine. The Greeks believed that wine was a gift from Dionysus, the god of wine, fertility, and theater. They pioneered the concept of terroir, understanding that the characteristics of the land, climate, and soil where grapes were grown significantly influenced the quality and flavor of the wine. Greek vintners experimented with different grape varieties and winemaking techniques, laying the foundation for many modern practices.

The Romans inherited and further refined the viticultural knowledge of the Greeks. They were passionate about wine and made it an integral part of their daily lives, from lavish banquets to religious ceremonies. The Roman Empire's vast reach facilitated the spread of viticulture across Europe. The Romans introduced advanced winemaking techniques, such as the use of sulfur dioxide to preserve wine and the development of wooden barrels for aging and storage. Their texts, like Pliny the Elder's "Natural History," provide invaluable insights into ancient winemaking practices and grape varieties.

Roman viticulture reached its zenith with the establishment of large-scale vineyards and the production of wines that were celebrated throughout the empire. The Romans recognized the importance of location in viticulture and classified vineyards according to their quality, a precursor to modern appellations. They also developed sophisticated methods for training and pruning vines, techniques that are still in use today. The fall of the Roman Empire led to a decline in viticulture in Western Europe, but the knowledge and traditions of winemaking were preserved by the Christian monastic orders.

Throughout the Middle Ages, monasteries became the custodians of viticultural knowledge. Monks meticulously tended vineyards and produced wines for sacramental use and sustenance. The Benedictine and Cistercian orders were particularly influential, establishing vineyards in regions that remain famous for wine production today, such as Burgundy and Champagne in France. These monastic communities maintained detailed records of their winemaking activities, contributing to the preservation and advancement of viticultural practices.

The history of wine is also marked by its cultural significance. Throughout the ages, wine has been associated with celebration, ritual, and social bonding. In ancient societies, wine was often consumed in communal settings, reinforcing social ties and facilitating communication. It played a central role in religious ceremonies, from the libations poured in honor of the gods to the Eucharistic wine used in Christian liturgy. The symbolic power of wine is evident in literature and art, where it frequently appears as a motif representing life, fertility, and divine favor.

Key historical figures have also left their mark on the history of wine. In ancient Greece, Theophrastus, a student of Aristotle, wrote extensively about viticulture in his botanical works. His observations on grapevine cultivation and the effects of climate and soil on wine quality were remarkably advanced for his time. In Rome, the agronomist Columella authored "De Re Rustica," an influential treatise on agriculture that includes detailed instructions on vineyard management and winemaking. These early scholars laid the groundwork for the scientific study of viticulture and oenology.

Wine in the Middle Ages

The Middle Ages, spanning roughly from the 5th to the late 15th century, were a transformative period for viticulture and winemaking in Europe. During this time, wine evolved from a luxury of the elite to a staple beverage consumed by various social classes. The era was marked by significant advancements in viticultural techniques, the establishment of wine-growing regions, and the profound influence of the Church on wine production and consumption.

Following the fall of the Roman Empire, Europe entered a period of political fragmentation and instability. Despite these challenges, the tradition of winemaking persisted, primarily within monastic communities. Monasteries became the primary centers for viticulture and oenology. Monks meticulously tended vineyards, documented their methods, and improved upon ancient techniques. The Benedictine and Cistercian orders were particularly influential, establishing vineyards across Europe, including in regions such as Burgundy, Champagne, and the Rhine Valley.

Monasteries were ideal places for viticulture due to their stability and relative wealth. The monks' commitment to discipline and routine was well-suited to the demands of vineyard management. They kept detailed records of their agricultural practices, including the types of grapes grown, planting and pruning schedules, and winemaking processes. These records not only preserved ancient knowledge but also facilitated the transmission of viticultural expertise across generations and regions.

One of the most significant contributions of the monastic orders was the identification and development of specific wine-growing regions. The monks recognized that certain areas produced superior grapes and, consequently, better wine. This understanding laid the groundwork for the concept of terroir, which holds that the unique combination of soil, climate, and topography of a region imparts distinct characteristics to its wine. Burgundy, for instance, owes much of its reputation to the meticulous vineyard practices established by the Cistercian monks.

The Church's influence extended beyond the vineyards. Wine was integral to the Christian liturgy, particularly in the celebration of the Eucharist. This religious significance ensured that wine production continued even during periods of economic and social turmoil. The demand for sacramental wine provided a steady market, supporting the continued cultivation of vineyards and the refinement of winemaking techniques.

As monastic viticulture flourished, secular vineyards also began to emerge, particularly in the burgeoning urban centers of medieval Europe. Nobles and wealthy merchants established their own vineyards, often employing the expertise of monastic vintners. The rise of feudalism saw the proliferation of vineyards on estates, with lords granting land to vassals in exchange for a portion of the wine produced.

The medieval period also witnessed the development of new grape varieties and the introduction of vines to previously untapped regions. The spread of Christianity played a crucial role in this expansion, as missionaries carried vines and viticultural knowledge with them as they traveled. For example, the spread of the Benedictine order brought viticulture to regions such as Germany, where the monks cultivated the now-renowned Riesling grape.

Trade and commerce during the Middle Ages significantly impacted the wine industry. The growth of cities and the establishment of trade routes facilitated the exchange of wine across Europe. Wine from regions like Bordeaux, Burgundy, and the Rhineland became highly sought after, and merchants played a central role in distributing these wines far and wide. The Hanseatic League, a powerful commercial alliance of merchant guilds and market towns in Northwestern and Central Europe, was instrumental in the trade of Rhenish wines throughout the Baltic and North Sea regions.

The medieval wine trade was not without its challenges. Transporting wine over long distances posed significant risks, including spoilage and theft. To mitigate these risks, merchants developed various preservation techniques. One common method was to add herbs and spices to the wine, both to enhance flavor and to act as preservatives. Another practice was aging wine in barrels, a technique that not only improved the wine's longevity but also imparted unique flavors from the wood.

The regulation of wine production and trade became increasingly important during the Middle Ages. Local governments and guilds established rules to ensure the quality and authenticity of wine. In some regions, specific laws dictated how and when grapes could be harvested, the methods of production, and the standards for aging and storage. These regulations helped maintain the reputation of regional wines and protected consumers from fraudulent practices.

Wine consumption during the Middle Ages varied widely depending on social status and geographic location. For the nobility and wealthy merchants, wine was a symbol of status and sophistication. Lavish feasts often featured a variety of wines, with the finest vintages reserved for the most honored guests. In contrast, the lower classes typically consumed simpler, locally-produced wines. In many parts of Europe, wine was a daily beverage, consumed with meals and often diluted with water. This practice was partly due to the poor quality of drinking water, making wine a safer alternative.

Wine also played a role in medieval medicine. It was commonly used as a base for medicinal concoctions, infused with herbs and spices believed to have healing properties. Physicians of the time prescribed wine for a variety of ailments, from digestive issues to wounds and infections. The warming and soothing properties of wine were thought to balance the body's humors, a central concept in medieval medicine.

The cultural significance of wine in the Middle Ages is evident in the art and literature of the period. Manuscripts, tapestries, and paintings frequently depicted scenes of vineyard labor, wine consumption, and festive gatherings. Works of literature, such as the epic poems of the troubadours and the tales of Chaucer, often featured wine as a symbol of celebration, hospitality, and social cohesion.

The legacy of medieval viticulture and winemaking is profound. The techniques and traditions developed during this period laid the foundation for modern practices. The emphasis on terroir, the meticulous care of the vines, and the importance of wine in social and religious life have all endured. The monastic vineyards, many of which continue to produce wine today, stand as a testament to the enduring influence of the Middle Ages on the world of wine.

The Evolution of Modern Winemaking

The evolution of modern winemaking is a fascinating journey that intertwines tradition, innovation, and science. From the late 19th century to the present day, winemaking has undergone significant transformations, driven by technological advancements, scientific discoveries, and a deeper understanding of viticulture and oenology. This chapter delves into the key developments and innovations that have shaped contemporary winemaking, highlighting the milestones that have revolutionized the industry and the practices that continue to define it.

The late 19th century marked a turning point in winemaking with the advent of phylloxera, a devastating vine pest that nearly decimated European vineyards. This crisis led to the discovery of grafting European grapevines onto resistant American rootstocks, a practice that saved the viticulture industry and remains a standard procedure today. The phylloxera epidemic also spurred scientific research into plant pathology and viticulture, fostering a more systematic approach to vineyard management.

As winemakers grappled with phylloxera, advancements in fermentation science began to take shape. The work of Louis Pasteur in the mid-19th century had profound implications for winemaking. Pasteur's studies on fermentation and microbial activity elucidated the role of yeast in converting grape sugars into alcohol, laying the groundwork for controlled fermentation processes. Understanding the microbiology of fermentation allowed winemakers to manage and optimize this critical stage, improving consistency and quality in wine production.

The 20th century witnessed a series of technological innovations that further transformed winemaking. The introduction of stainless steel tanks revolutionized fermentation and storage, offering a hygienic and inert alternative to traditional wooden vats. Stainless steel's temperature control capabilities enabled precise regulation of fermentation conditions, enhancing the retention of fresh fruit flavors and aromatic compounds, particularly in white wines. This technology also facilitated the production of clean, crisp wines with minimal risk of contamination.

Temperature control extended beyond fermentation to other stages of winemaking. The development of refrigeration technology allowed winemakers to control temperatures during grape harvesting, transportation, and storage. This innovation was particularly crucial for regions with warm climates, where temperature fluctuations could negatively impact grape quality. By maintaining optimal temperatures, winemakers could preserve the integrity of the grapes and produce wines with greater finesse and balance.

The mid-20th century also saw the rise of modern enology, the science of winemaking. Research institutions and universities established dedicated programs to study viticulture and enology, fostering a new generation of winemakers with a scientific approach to their craft. The application of chemistry, biology, and engineering principles to winemaking led to a deeper understanding of the processes involved and the factors influencing wine quality. This scientific foundation enabled winemakers to experiment with new techniques and technologies, pushing the boundaries of traditional practices.

One of the most significant advancements in modern winemaking is the development of controlled malolactic fermentation (MLF). This secondary fermentation process, in which lactic acid bacteria convert sharp malic acid to softer lactic acid, has become a standard practice for many red wines and some white wines. Controlled MLF can enhance mouthfeel, complexity, and stability, allowing winemakers to fine-tune the sensory profile of their wines. The ability to induce or inhibit MLF with precision has given winemakers greater flexibility in crafting their desired style.

The late 20th and early 21st centuries have seen the integration of precision viticulture into modern winemaking. This approach leverages technology such as satellite imagery, GPS, and soil sensors to monitor and manage vineyard conditions with unprecedented accuracy. Precision viticulture allows for the identification of variations within a vineyard, enabling targeted interventions such as irrigation, fertilization, and pest control. By optimizing vineyard management practices, winemakers can enhance grape quality and achieve greater consistency across vintages.

Advancements in grape harvesting technology have also played a crucial role in modern winemaking. Mechanical harvesters, equipped with sensors and sorting mechanisms, have become increasingly sophisticated, allowing for efficient and selective harvesting. These machines can operate at night, taking advantage of cooler temperatures to preserve grape freshness. While hand harvesting remains preferred for certain premium wines, mechanical harvesting has become a valuable tool for many winemakers, particularly in large-scale operations.

The rise of organic and biodynamic viticulture represents another significant evolution in modern winemaking. As consumer demand for sustainable and environmentally friendly products has grown, many winemakers have embraced organic and biodynamic practices. Organic viticulture eschews synthetic chemicals in favor of natural alternatives, promoting biodiversity and soil health. Biodynamic viticulture, based on the principles of Rudolph Steiner, incorporates holistic and spiritual elements, emphasizing the interconnectedness of the vineyard ecosystem. These practices not only appeal to eco-conscious consumers but also contribute to the long-term sustainability of vineyards.

The influence of globalization on winemaking cannot be overlooked. The exchange of knowledge, technology, and expertise across wine regions has fostered a more interconnected and innovative industry. Winemakers travel, collaborate, and learn from one another, adopting best practices and experimenting with new techniques. This cross-pollination has led to the emergence of new wine styles and the revitalization of traditional ones, enriching the diversity and complexity of the global wine landscape.

Modern winemaking has also been profoundly shaped by advances in analytical chemistry. The ability to analyze grape and wine composition with precision has revolutionized quality control and wine characterization. Techniques such as gas chromatography, mass spectrometry, and spectroscopy allow winemakers to monitor and manipulate the levels of various compounds that influence flavor, aroma, and stability. This analytical prowess has enabled winemakers to create wines with greater consistency, complexity, and age-worthiness.

The rise of consumer-centric winemaking has transformed how wines are produced and marketed. Winemakers have become increasingly attuned to consumer preferences, using market research and sensory analysis to guide their decisions. This approach has led to the development of wine styles and brands tailored to specific demographics and tastes. The proliferation of wine tourism and direct-to-consumer sales channels has further strengthened the connection between winemakers and their customers, fostering loyalty and engagement.

Sustainability has become a cornerstone of modern winemaking. Climate change, resource scarcity, and environmental degradation have prompted winemakers to adopt more sustainable practices. Water conservation, renewable energy, and waste reduction are now integral to many wineries' operations. Certification programs, such as organic, biodynamic, and sustainable winegrowing, provide consumers with assurances of environmentally responsible practices. The commitment to sustainability not only addresses ecological concerns but also enhances the resilience and longevity of vineyards.

Innovation in packaging has also left its mark on modern winemaking. The traditional glass bottle, while still dominant, is now complemented by alternative packaging options such as bag-in-box, Tetra Pak, and aluminum cans. These options offer benefits in terms of cost, convenience, and environmental impact. For example, bag-in-box packaging reduces transportation weight and carbon emissions, while aluminum cans are lightweight, recyclable, and ideal for on-the-go consumption. These innovations have expanded the accessibility and appeal of wine to a broader audience.

As we look to the future, the evolution of modern winemaking continues unabated. Emerging technologies, such as artificial intelligence, robotics, and blockchain, hold the potential to further revolutionize the industry. AI-driven vineyard management systems can optimize every aspect of viticulture, from disease detection to yield prediction. Robotics can automate labor-intensive tasks, improving efficiency and precision. Blockchain technology can enhance traceability and transparency, providing consumers with detailed information about the provenance and production of their wine.

Wine's Cultural Significance

Wine's cultural significance stretches back millennia, intertwined with the history, religion, and social customs of civilizations around the world. Its journey from a simple fermented beverage to a symbol of status and ritual is a testament to its profound impact on human society. This chapter explores the multifaceted role wine has played across different eras and cultures, illustrating its enduring importance and the diverse meanings it has acquired along the way.

The earliest known wine production dates back to around 6000 BCE in what is now Georgia. Archaeological evidence, such as ancient pottery with wine residues, suggests that early humans quickly recognized the value of fermented grapes. The ancients didn't just drink wine for its intoxicating effects; it was also used in religious and ceremonial contexts. In Mesopotamia, for instance, wine was offered to gods in rituals, symbolizing a connection between the divine and the mortal.

Moving westward to ancient Egypt, wine was a staple in the tombs of pharaohs, intended to accompany them into the afterlife. The Egyptians believed wine had magical and life-sustaining properties. It was often depicted in tomb paintings, showing scenes of grape harvesting and winemaking, underscoring its significance in daily and spiritual life. The consumption of wine was initially reserved for the elite, reflecting its status as a luxury item.

The Greeks further elevated wine's cultural status. Not only did they perfect the art of viticulture, but they also integrated wine into their social and philosophical lives. Symposia, social gatherings where intellectuals discussed philosophy and politics over wine, became a hallmark of Greek culture. Dionysus, the Greek god of wine, represented both the joy and chaos that wine could bring, embodying its dual nature. The Greeks also pioneered the concept of terroir, recognizing that the quality of wine was influenced by the specific characteristics of the land where the grapes were grown.

Roman society inherited and expanded upon Greek traditions, spreading viticulture across Europe. Wine became a daily staple for Romans of all classes, often consumed diluted with water. The Roman god Bacchus, akin to Dionysus, was central to festivals and bacchanals, events characterized by wild revelry and excessive drinking. However, the Romans also appreciated the finer aspects of wine, collecting and aging it, and establishing some of the earliest wine classifications based on quality and origin.

In medieval Europe, wine took on new dimensions of cultural significance, particularly within the Christian church. The sacrament of the Eucharist, wherein wine symbolizes the blood of Christ, became a central ritual in Christian worship. Monasteries became key centers of wine production, preserving and advancing viticultural knowledge through the Middle Ages. Monks meticulously tended vineyards, producing wine for religious ceremonies and, increasingly, for commerce. This period also saw the rise of wine as a social staple in European courts and among the burgeoning merchant class, signaling a shift from purely sacred to secular enjoyment.

The Renaissance brought a renewed appreciation for classical learning and, with it, an elevated status for wine. As European explorers ventured to the New World, they carried vines with them, spreading viticulture to places like South America and California. Wine began to symbolize not just wealth and sophistication but also the spread of European culture and influence. This era laid the groundwork for the global wine industry we recognize today.

In more recent history, the cultural significance of wine has continued to evolve. The 19th and 20th centuries saw the rise of wine as a symbol of national identity, particularly in countries like France, Italy, and Spain. Appellations and controlled designations of origin were established to protect the unique qualities of wines from specific regions. This period also marked the democratization of wine, making it accessible to a broader audience, though it still retained an air of sophistication and exclusivity.

Contemporary wine culture is a tapestry of these historical threads, woven with new patterns of globalism and diversity. Wine tourism has become a significant industry, with regions like Napa Valley, Bordeaux, and Tuscany attracting millions of visitors annually These regions not only offer wine tasting but also a cultural immersion into the traditions and landscapes that produce these renowned wines. Wine festivals, such as Oktoberfest in Munich or the Haro Wine Festival in Spain, celebrate the joyous and communal aspects of wine drinking, drawing people from all walks of life.

The rise of the sommelier profession has also highlighted wine's cultural significance in modern times. Sommeliers are more than just wine stewards; they are educators and ambassadors of wine culture, guiding consumers through the vast and complex world of wine with expertise and passion. Their role underscores the continuing evolution of wine appreciation, blending deep knowledge with a celebration of sensory experience.

Moreover, wine has found a place in the arts and media, further cementing its cultural footprint. Films like "Sideways" and documentaries such as "Somm" explore the nuances of wine culture and its impact on personal and social identity. Literature, too, has long celebrated wine, from the ancient poetry of Omar Khayyam to the modern musings of wine critics and aficionados.

In the realm of gastronomy, wine has become an essential component, enhancing and complementing culinary creations. The concept of food and wine pairing, though ancient, has reached new heights with contemporary chefs and sommeliers collaborating to create harmonious dining experiences. This synergy between food and wine underscores the cultural importance of wine as a companion to human celebration and connection.

Wine's role in social and political movements cannot be overlooked. In the 20th century, the prohibition era in the United States highlighted the contentious nature of alcohol consumption and its deep-rooted place in society. The eventual repeal of prohibition reaffirmed wine's cultural significance, leading to a resurgence of American winemaking. Similarly, movements advocating for organic and biodynamic winemaking practices reflect broader societal concerns about sustainability and environmental stewardship, positioning wine production within the context of global ecological consciousness.

In contemporary society, wine continues to evolve, mirroring changes in social norms and values. The increasing popularity of natural wines, which emphasize minimal intervention and traditional methods, reflects a growing consumer desire for authenticity and transparency. This trend is part of a broader cultural shift towards valuing artisanal and locally-sourced products, highlighting wine's ability to adapt and remain relevant in changing times.

Key Historical Figures in Oenology

Oenology, the study of wine and winemaking, has been shaped by numerous influential figures throughout history. These individuals have contributed significantly to our understanding of viticulture, the chemistry of wine, and the art of winemaking. Their legacies continue to influence modern practices and innovations in the field. This chapter delves into the lives and contributions of some key historical figures in oenology, highlighting their lasting impact on the world of wine.

One of the earliest known figures in the history of winemaking is Hesiod, an ancient Greek poet who lived around 700 BCE. In his works, "Works and Days" and "Theogony," Hesiod provided detailed descriptions of agricultural practices, including viticulture. His writings offer a glimpse into early Greek methods of grape cultivation and wine production, emphasizing the importance of timing and climate. Hesiod's attention to detail and his understanding of the agricultural cycles laid the groundwork for future advancements in viticulture.

Moving forward in time, the Roman author and naturalist Pliny the Elder made significant contributions to the field of oenology. His encyclopedic work, "Natural History," written in the first century CE, includes extensive information on grape varieties, wine regions, and winemaking techniques. Pliny's observations on the influence of terroir on wine quality were particularly insightful, and his classification of wines from different regions provided a foundation for the concept of appellations. Pliny's work remains a valuable resource for understanding ancient Roman viticulture and winemaking.

During the Middle Ages, wine production and knowledge were preserved and advanced by monastic communities. One of the most notable figures from this period is Dom Pierre Pérignon, a Benedictine monk who lived in the late 17th and early 18th centuries. Often credited with the invention of Champagne, Dom Pérignon's contributions to the field are both legendary and transformative. He developed techniques for blending different grape varieties to achieve balance and complexity, and he refined the méthode champenoise, the traditional method of producing sparkling wine. While the myths surrounding his role in the creation of Champagne may be embellished, there is no doubt that Dom Pérignon's innovations had a lasting impact on the production of sparkling wine.

In the 19th century, the field of oenology saw significant advancements thanks to the work of Louis Pasteur. A French microbiologist and chemist, Pasteur's research on fermentation and the role of yeast was groundbreaking. His discovery that microorganisms were responsible for fermentation helped demystify the process and provided a scientific basis for winemaking. Pasteur's work also led to the development of pasteurization, a method of controlling microbial activity in wine and other beverages. His contributions to microbiology and chemistry revolutionized the wine industry, making winemaking more predictable and consistent.

The late 19th and early 20th centuries witnessed the rise of another influential figure in oenology, Émile Peynaud. Often referred to as the father of modern oenology, Peynaud was a French enologist and professor who brought a scientific approach to winemaking. His book, "The Taste of Wine," published in 1983, is considered a seminal work in the field. Peynaud emphasized the importance of controlling fermentation temperatures, using stainless steel tanks, and implementing rigorous hygiene practices in the winery. His teachings and research helped winemakers produce higher quality wines with greater consistency, and his influence can still be seen in contemporary winemaking techniques.

In the realm of viticulture, Dr. Harold Olmo, an American viticulturist, made significant contributions during the 20th century. A professor at the University of California, Davis, Olmo dedicated his career to breeding grape varieties that were resistant to diseases and pests. His work led to the development of numerous grape varieties that are now widely planted in vineyards around the world. Olmo's research on climate adaptation and vineyard management practices also helped viticulturists optimize grape growing conditions, enhancing the quality and resilience of vineyards.

Another key figure in the history of oenology is André Tchelistcheff, a Russian-born enologist who became one of the most influential winemakers in California. Tchelistcheff's impact on the American wine industry is profound. He introduced modern winemaking techniques, such as cold fermentation and malolactic fermentation, which improved the quality and stability of wines. Tchelistcheff's mentorship of numerous winemakers and his role in establishing Napa Valley as a premier wine region have left a lasting legacy on the American wine scene.

In more recent times, the contributions of Jancis Robinson, a British wine critic, journalist, and author, have been invaluable to the field of oenology. Robinson's extensive writings on wine, including "The Oxford Companion to Wine" and "Wine Grapes," have become essential references for wine professionals and enthusiasts alike. Her rigorous research, clear writing style, and comprehensive knowledge have helped demystify the world of wine for a broad audience. Robinson's influence extends beyond her publications, as she has been an advocate for transparent labeling and sustainable practices in the wine industry.

The late 20th and early 21st centuries have also seen the rise of influential figures such as Robert Parker, an American wine critic whose publication, "The Wine Advocate," has had a significant impact on the global wine market. Parker's 100-point rating system revolutionized wine criticism, providing consumers with a straightforward way to evaluate and compare wines. While his influence has been a subject of debate, there is no denying that Parker's reviews have shaped the perceptions and buying habits of wine consumers worldwide.

As we look to the future, the field of oenology continues to evolve, with new figures emerging to push the boundaries of winemaking and viticulture. Pioneers in the study of climate change, such as Dr. Gregory Jones, are exploring how shifting weather patterns affect grape growing and wine production. Their research is crucial for developing strategies to adapt to changing conditions and ensure the sustainability of the wine industry.

Chapter 2

Understanding the Vineyard

Viticulture Basics

Understanding the fundamentals of viticulture is essential for anyone interested in the art and science of grape growing. Viticulture, the cultivation and harvesting of grapes, is a complex and nuanced field that requires knowledge of plant biology, soil science, climate, and meticulous vineyard management practices. This chapter outlines the basic principles of viticulture, providing a solid foundation for beginners and enthusiasts alike.

Viticulture begins with the selection of the site for the vineyard. The location of the vineyard plays a critical role in determining the quality and characteristics of the grapes produced. Factors such as climate, soil type, topography, and exposure to sunlight all influence grape growth and development. The ideal site has a balance of these elements, providing the vines with the necessary conditions to thrive. For instance, regions with a temperate climate and well-draining soils are typically preferred for grape cultivation. The slope and orientation of the land can also impact the amount of sunlight the vines receive, which is crucial for photosynthesis and ripening.

Once the site is selected, the next step is choosing the grape varieties to plant. There are thousands of grape varieties, each with unique characteristics and suitability for different climates and soils. The choice of grape variety depends on several factors, including the intended style of wine, market demand, and local growing conditions. For example, Cabernet Sauvignon and Chardonnay are popular choices for their versatility and adaptability to various climates. Understanding the specific requirements and traits of each grape variety is essential for successful viticulture.

Planting the vineyard involves careful planning and execution. The layout of the vineyard, including row spacing and vine density, affects the overall health and productivity of the vines. Proper spacing ensures that each vine receives adequate sunlight and air circulation, reducing the risk of disease and promoting even ripening. The choice of rootstock is also important, as it provides the foundation for the vine and influences its vigor and resistance to pests and diseases. Selecting the appropriate rootstock for the soil and climate conditions can enhance the vineyard's resilience and longevity.

Soil management is a critical aspect of viticulture. The soil provides the essential nutrients and water that the vines need to grow. Different soil types, such as sandy, clay, or loamy soils, have varying capacities for water retention and nutrient availability. Understanding the soil composition and structure helps in implementing appropriate management practices. Regular soil testing can identify nutrient deficiencies or imbalances, allowing for targeted fertilization and amendments. Organic matter, such as compost or cover crops, can improve soil structure and fertility, promoting healthy vine growth.

Water management is another key component of viticulture. Grapevines require a consistent supply of water, especially during the growing season. However, over-watering can lead to problems such as root rot and reduced fruit quality. The goal is to provide enough water to sustain the vines without causing stress or waterlogging. Irrigation practices, such as drip irrigation, are commonly used to deliver water directly to the root zone, minimizing waste and ensuring efficient water use. Monitoring soil moisture levels and understanding the water needs of the vines at different growth stages are essential for effective water management.

Pest and disease management is crucial for maintaining a healthy vineyard. Grapevines are susceptible to various pests and diseases, including insects, fungi, bacteria, and viruses. Integrated pest management (IPM) is a holistic approach that combines cultural, biological, and chemical methods to control pests and diseases. Regular monitoring and early detection are key components of IPM, allowing for timely interventions and minimizing the use of chemical pesticides. Biological controls, such as beneficial insects or microbial agents, can help manage pest populations naturally. Additionally, cultural practices, such as canopy management and sanitation, reduce the risk of disease outbreaks by improving air circulation and removing infected plant material.

Canopy management involves the strategic pruning and training of grapevines to optimize sunlight exposure, air circulation, and fruit development. Proper canopy management enhances photosynthesis, reduces disease pressure, and ensures uniform ripening of the grapes. Techniques such as leaf removal, shoot thinning, and trellising are used to achieve the desired canopy structure. The goal is to create an open and balanced canopy that supports healthy vine growth and high-quality fruit production.

Harvesting is a critical stage in the viticulture process. The timing of the harvest significantly impacts the quality and style of the wine. Grapes are typically harvested when they reach optimal ripeness, determined by factors such as sugar content, acidity, and flavor development. The decision to harvest involves careful monitoring of these parameters and can vary depending on the grape variety and desired wine style. Hand harvesting is often preferred for premium wines, as it allows for selective picking and minimizes damage to the grapes. Mechanical harvesting, while more efficient, may be suitable for larger vineyards and certain wine styles.

Post-harvest practices, such as sorting and handling, are also important for maintaining grape quality. Sorting involves removing any damaged or unripe grapes, ensuring that only the best fruit is used for winemaking. Gentle handling and transport of the grapes to the winery minimize bruising and oxidation, preserving the integrity of the fruit.

Sustainable viticulture practices are becoming increasingly important in the industry. Sustainable viticulture aims to balance economic viability with environmental stewardship and social responsibility. This approach involves practices that conserve natural resources, protect biodiversity, and reduce the environmental impact of vineyard operations. Techniques such as organic farming, biodynamic practices, and the use of renewable energy are gaining popularity among grape growers. These practices not only benefit the environment but also contribute to the long-term health and productivity of the vineyard.

Education and continuous learning are vital for success in viticulture. The field is constantly evolving, with new research and technologies emerging. Staying informed about the latest advancements and best practices can help viticulturists make informed decisions and improve their vineyard management. Participating in industry workshops, conferences, and networking with other professionals provides valuable insights and opportunities for learning. Additionally, maintaining detailed records of vineyard activities, such as soil tests, pest management, and weather conditions, can aid in evaluating and refining practices over time.

Grape Varieties

Grape varieties, also known as cultivars, are the cornerstone of viticulture and winemaking. Each variety possesses unique characteristics that define the flavor, aroma, and overall profile of the wine it produces. Understanding the diversity and specific attributes of different grape varieties is essential for any aspiring viticulturist or wine enthusiast. This chapter delves into the world of grape varieties, offering insights into their origins, traits, and the factors influencing their cultivation.

The story of grape varieties begins thousands of
years ago, with the domestication of the wild grape
species Vitis vinifera. Over time, human intervention
and natural selection led to the development of
numerous cultivars, each adapted to specific climates
and regions. Today, there are over 10,000 known
grape varieties, though only a fraction are widely
cultivated for wine production.

One of the most important factors in choosing a
grape variety is the climate of the vineyard location.
Grapes are highly sensitive to temperature, and
different varieties thrive in different climatic
conditions. For example, cool-climate varieties such
as Pinot Noir and Riesling prefer regions with
moderate temperatures and long growing seasons.
These varieties develop complex flavors and retain
high acidity, making them ideal for producing
elegant, balanced wines. On the other hand, warm-
climate varieties like Syrah and Zinfandel flourish in
hotter regions, where they achieve full ripeness and
produce rich, robust wines with higher alcohol
content.

Soil type is another critical factor influencing grape
variety selection. The composition, drainage, and
fertility of the soil affect vine growth and grape
quality. For instance, Chardonnay thrives in chalky,
limestone-rich soils, which contribute to the wine's
minerality and crispness. Bordeaux varieties such as

Cabernet Sauvignon and Merlot are well-suited to gravelly soils, which provide excellent drainage and moderate vine vigor, resulting in concentrated, flavorful grapes.

Grape varieties also exhibit distinct morphological and physiological traits that impact their cultivation and management. These traits include vine vigor, cluster size and shape, berry size, and susceptibility to diseases. For example, Pinot Noir is known for its tight clusters and thin skins, making it prone to diseases like botrytis bunch rot. This sensitivity requires meticulous vineyard management practices, such as leaf removal and careful monitoring of humidity levels, to prevent disease outbreaks. Conversely, Cabernet Sauvignon has thick skins and loose clusters, which provide better resistance to pests and diseases, making it a more robust and easier-to-manage variety.

The sensory characteristics of grape varieties are perhaps their most defining feature. Each variety has a unique combination of flavors, aromas, and textures that contribute to the wine's identity. For example, Sauvignon Blanc is renowned for its vibrant acidity and distinctive aromas of citrus, green apple, and grassy notes. In contrast, Merlot is celebrated for its smooth texture and flavors of plum, black cherry, and chocolate. These sensory attributes are influenced by the grape's genetic makeup, growing conditions, and winemaking techniques.

Classic grape varieties, often referred to as noble varieties, have a long history of producing high-quality wines and are widely recognized around the world. These include varieties such as Cabernet Sauvignon, Merlot, Pinot Noir, Chardonnay, Sauvignon Blanc, and Riesling. These noble varieties have proven their versatility and adaptability to various terroirs, making them popular choices for winemakers seeking to produce premium wines.

Emerging and lesser-known grape varieties are also gaining attention in the viticulture community. These varieties often possess unique qualities and offer opportunities for innovation and differentiation in the wine market. For example, Tannat, originally from the Madiran region of France, is known for its deep color, high tannin content, and aging potential. It has gained popularity in Uruguay, where it produces bold, structured wines that reflect the country's terroir. Similarly, Grüner Veltliner, a white variety from Austria, is celebrated for its fresh acidity, subtle spice, and versatility with food pairings.

The concept of terroir, which encompasses the environmental factors influencing grape growing, plays a significant role in shaping the character of grape varieties. Terroir includes elements such as climate, soil, topography, and human intervention. The interaction between these factors and the grape variety results in wines that express the unique qualities of their origin. For example, the same grape variety planted in different regions can produce wines with distinct characteristics. A Chardonnay from Burgundy may exhibit mineral and citrus notes, while a Chardonnay from California might display tropical fruit flavors and a fuller body.

Clonal selection is another important aspect of grape variety cultivation. Clonal selection involves identifying and propagating vines with desirable traits, such as disease resistance, yield, or specific flavor profiles. This practice helps maintain the genetic diversity and health of grapevine populations while optimizing vineyard performance. For example, in the case of Pinot Noir, numerous clones have been developed, each with unique attributes that contribute to the complexity and diversity of Pinot Noir wines.

The choice of grape variety also influences vineyard management practices, including pruning, canopy management, and harvest timing. Different varieties have varying growth habits and ripening patterns, requiring tailored approaches to maximize grape quality. For instance, Syrah benefits from aggressive pruning to control its vigorous growth, while Riesling requires careful canopy management to protect the grapes from sunburn and maintain acidity.

Sustainability and resilience in grape variety selection are becoming increasingly important in the face of climate change and environmental challenges. Grape growers are exploring varieties that are more adaptable to changing conditions and require fewer inputs such as water, pesticides, and fertilizers. For example, Mediterranean varieties like Grenache and Vermentino are gaining popularity in regions experiencing warmer and drier conditions due to their drought tolerance and ability to produce high-quality wines under stress.

Grape variety diversity also plays a role in preserving cultural heritage and promoting biodiversity. Many indigenous and heirloom varieties, which have been cultivated for centuries in specific regions, are being rediscovered and celebrated for their historical significance and unique qualities. These varieties often have deep cultural ties and offer a connection to the past, enriching the tapestry of the global wine industry.

Terroir and Its Importance

Terroir, a term deeply rooted in French winemaking culture, encapsulates the essence of a wine's sense of place. It encompasses the myriad environmental factors that influence grape growing, including soil, climate, topography, and even human intervention. Understanding terroir is crucial for anyone looking to delve into viticulture or wine appreciation, as it is these factors that impart unique characteristics and flavors to wines from different regions.

The concept of terroir begins with the soil. Soil composition can vary dramatically from one vineyard to another, affecting the type of grape that can be grown and the quality of the wine produced. Soils rich in limestone, such as those found in Burgundy, France, are known to produce wines with high acidity and longevity. In contrast, the volcanic soils in regions like Mount Etna in Sicily contribute to wines with distinct minerality and complexity. The drainage capacity of the soil also plays a role; well-drained soils encourage deep root systems, promoting vine health and resilience.

Climate is another pivotal component of terroir. It encompasses both macroclimate (the broader regional climate) and microclimate (the specific climatic conditions of a particular vineyard). Cool-climate regions like the Loire Valley in France or the Willamette Valley in Oregon are known for producing wines with higher acidity and more subtle, nuanced flavors. Grapes in these regions ripen slowly, allowing for the development of complex aromatics. On the other hand, warm-climate regions such as California's Napa Valley yield wines that are often richer, with higher alcohol levels and more pronounced fruit flavors due to the greater accumulation of sugars in the grapes.

Topography, or the physical landscape of a vineyard, further defines the terroir. Factors such as altitude, slope, and aspect (the direction a vineyard faces) influence grape ripening and, consequently, wine characteristics. Vineyards at higher altitudes, like those in Argentina's Mendoza region, benefit from cooler temperatures and increased diurnal temperature variation, which helps preserve acidity while allowing grapes to develop intense flavors. Slopes facilitate drainage and reduce the risk of frost, while aspect determines the amount of sunlight vines receive, impacting photosynthesis and grape maturation. intervention, often termed the "hand of the winemaker," is the final element of terroir. While terroir is predominantly about natural factors, the decisions made by viticulturists and winemakers significantly shape the expression of terroir in the final wine. Choices around vine training systems, pruning, harvest timing, and winemaking techniques such as fermentation and aging methods can enhance or obscure the natural characteristics imparted by soil, climate, and topography.

The interplay of these elements creates a unique signature for each vineyard, making terroir a vital consideration in the production of high-quality wines. For instance, the chalky soils and cool climate of Champagne contribute to the region's renowned sparkling wines, characterized by their finesse, acidity, and minerality. In contrast, the warm, sunny climate and diverse soils of the Rhône Valley result in robust, full-bodied reds with rich fruit flavors and spicy undertones.

Terroir also plays a critical role in the concept of appellations, which are legally defined and regulated geographical areas that produce wine under specific standards. These appellations, such as Bordeaux, Chianti, or Rioja, are often steeped in history and tradition, with strict regulations governing grape varieties, yields, and winemaking practices to preserve the unique identity of wines from these regions. Appellations serve as a guarantee of quality and authenticity, guiding consumers in their wine selections and helping to maintain the cultural heritage of winemaking regions.

Moreover, the importance of terroir extends beyond the sensory attributes of wine; it also has economic and cultural implications. Vineyards with a strong sense of terroir often command higher prices, as consumers and collectors seek out wines with distinctive character and provenance. This economic value supports local economies and incentivizes the preservation of traditional viticultural practices and landscapes. Culturally, terroir fosters a deep connection between winegrowers and their land, as well as between consumers and the regions they explore through wine. This connection is celebrated through wine tourism, festivals, and educational programs, which highlight the unique stories and heritage of winemaking regions.

In the context of a changing climate, the concept of terroir faces new challenges and opportunities. Climate change is altering temperature patterns, precipitation levels, and the frequency of extreme weather events, impacting grape growing conditions worldwide. Winemakers are adapting by exploring new grape varieties, adjusting vineyard practices, and even relocating vineyards to higher altitudes or cooler regions. These changes necessitate a re-evaluation of traditional notions of terroir, as the boundaries of suitable grape-growing areas shift and new expressions of terroir emerge. However, this also offers an opportunity for innovation and resilience, as the wine industry seeks to balance the preservation of heritage with the need for sustainability.

Understanding terroir is not just about recognizing the influence of environmental factors on wine; it is also about appreciating the artistry and craftsmanship involved in translating these factors into a bottle of wine. A winemaker's skill lies in interpreting the nuances of terroir and making decisions that best express the unique qualities of their vineyard. This might involve selecting the right grape variety for the soil and climate, choosing the optimal harvest time to capture the desired balance of ripeness and acidity, or employing specific fermentation techniques to highlight certain flavors and textures.

For wine enthusiasts, exploring the concept of terroir enhances the appreciation of wine on multiple levels. Tasting wines from different regions and understanding the characteristics of their terroir can reveal the diversity and complexity of the wine world. It also fosters a deeper connection to the land and the people who cultivate it, enriching the overall wine experience. Whether it's the flinty minerality of a Sancerre, the sun-soaked richness of a Napa Cabernet, or the earthy elegance of a Barolo, each wine tells a story of its origin, offering a glimpse into the unique interplay of nature and human ingenuity.

The Vineyard Lifecycle

The vineyard lifecycle is a journey of transformation, patience, and meticulous care, guiding grapevines from dormant winter buds to the bountiful harvests of late summer and early autumn. This cycle, steeped in tradition and science, dictates the rhythm of viticulture and the eventual quality of the wine produced. Understanding each stage of this lifecycle is essential for anyone venturing into grape growing or winemaking, as it provides the foundation for managing a vineyard and ensuring the health and productivity of the vines.

The lifecycle begins in the quiet of winter, a time of dormancy where vines rest and conserve energy. During this period, the vineyard appears lifeless, with bare canes and a stark landscape. However, this is a critical time for vineyard management. Pruning occurs in late winter, a precise and deliberate process that involves cutting back the previous year's growth to prepare the vine for the upcoming season. Pruning not only shapes the vine but also regulates the number of buds that will develop into fruit-bearing shoots, directly influencing the yield and quality of the grapes.

As winter gives way to spring, the vineyard awakens. Bud break marks the start of the growing season, typically occurring when temperatures consistently rise above 50°F (10°C). Small buds on the canes swell and eventually burst open, revealing tiny shoots and leaves. This is a vulnerable time for vines, as late frosts can damage the tender new growth. Vineyard managers often employ frost protection measures, such as wind machines or water sprinklers, to shield the young buds from freezing temperatures.

Spring progresses into early summer, and the vineyard enters the stage of rapid growth and flowering. The shoots elongate, leaves expand, and the vine's canopy fills out. Flowering usually occurs around 40 to 80 days after bud break, depending on the grape variety and climate. During this period, clusters of small, fragrant flowers bloom, which will eventually set into grape clusters. Successful pollination and fruit set are crucial, as poor weather conditions, such as rain or strong winds, can interfere with this process and reduce the potential yield.

Following flowering and fruit set, the vineyard enters a phase known as berry development. The tiny green berries that form after fruit set begin to grow and accumulate mass. This stage is marked by a rapid increase in size, primarily due to cell division and expansion. During this time, vineyard managers focus on canopy management practices, such as shoot thinning, leaf removal, and trellising, to ensure optimal sunlight exposure and air circulation for the developing grapes. These practices help prevent disease and promote even ripening.

As summer progresses, the grapes undergo a process called veraison, the onset of ripening. This is a visually striking phase where the berries change color—from green to red, purple, or golden, depending on the grape variety. Veraison signifies the transition from berry growth to berry ripening, where sugars accumulate, acids decrease, and flavor compounds develop. The timing of veraison can vary, but it generally occurs between mid-July and early August in the Northern Hemisphere. During this period, vineyard managers closely monitor the vines, adjusting irrigation and canopy management practices to support the ripening process.

The final stage of the vineyard lifecycle is the harvest, a culmination of the year's efforts. Harvest timing is critical, as the ripeness of the grapes directly impacts the wine's flavor, acidity, and alcohol content. Vineyard managers use a combination of sensory evaluation and scientific measurements, such as sugar levels (Brix), acidity, and pH, to determine the optimal harvest date. Depending on the grape variety and desired wine style, harvest can occur anywhere from late August to October. The grapes are carefully picked, either by hand or machine, and transported to the winery for processing.

Post-harvest, the vineyard enters a period of senescence, where the vines gradually shut down for the winter. Leaves change color and fall off, and the vines begin to store carbohydrates in their roots and trunks to sustain them through the dormant season. Vineyard managers take this time to conduct soil amendments, cover cropping, and other maintenance tasks to prepare for the next cycle.

Throughout the vineyard lifecycle, several key factors influence vine health and grape quality. Soil management is fundamental, as the soil provides the essential nutrients and water needed for vine growth. Vineyard managers regularly test soil composition and fertility, adjusting their practices to maintain a balanced and healthy soil environment. Cover crops, such as legumes and grasses, are often planted between vine rows to improve soil structure, prevent erosion, and promote beneficial microbial activity.

Water management is another critical aspect of the vineyard lifecycle. Vines require adequate water to support growth and grape development, but over-irrigation can lead to excessive vegetative growth and diluted flavors in the grapes. Vineyard managers use various irrigation techniques, such as drip irrigation or deficit irrigation, to provide the right amount of water at the right time. Monitoring soil moisture levels and weather conditions helps optimize irrigation practices and conserve water resources.

Pest and disease management is an ongoing concern throughout the vineyard lifecycle. Vines are susceptible to a range of pests, such as grapevine moths, mites, and nematodes, as well as diseases like powdery mildew, downy mildew, and botrytis bunch rot. Integrated pest management (IPM) strategies are employed to minimize the impact of these threats, combining biological controls, cultural practices, and chemical treatments when necessary. Regular monitoring and early intervention are key to maintaining vine health and preventing significant crop losses.

Climate and weather play a pivotal role in the vineyard lifecycle, influencing every stage from bud break to harvest. Temperature, rainfall, humidity, and sunlight all affect vine growth and grape ripening. Vineyard managers must be attuned to these factors, adapting their practices to mitigate adverse conditions and take advantage of favorable ones. Climate change is adding new challenges, with shifting weather patterns and increased occurrence of extreme events, such as heatwaves, droughts, and storms. Adaptation strategies, such as selecting drought-resistant rootstocks or altering vineyard orientation, are becoming increasingly important to ensure the sustainability of viticulture.

In addition to these practical aspects, the vineyard lifecycle is imbued with a sense of tradition and artistry. Winemaking regions around the world have developed unique practices and philosophies that reflect their cultural heritage and environmental conditions. From the terraced vineyards of Portugal's Douro Valley to the sun-drenched slopes of Australia's Barossa Valley, each region brings its own approach to managing the vineyard lifecycle. These traditions are passed down through generations, blending time-honored techniques with modern innovations to produce wines that express the character of their terroir.

Harvesting Grapes

Harvesting grapes is a momentous event in the vineyard lifecycle, marking the culmination of a year's worth of care and attention. This process, which involves much more than simply picking grapes from the vine, requires precision, timing, and a deep understanding of the vineyard's unique characteristics. The decisions made during harvest can significantly impact the quality of the wine, making it a critical stage in winemaking.

The timing of the harvest is perhaps the most crucial decision a vineyard manager will make. Grapes must be picked at the peak of ripeness to ensure the desired balance of sugar, acidity, and flavor compounds. This optimal ripeness varies depending on the grape variety, the style of wine being produced, and the specific conditions of the vineyard. Vineyard managers rely on a combination of scientific measurements and sensory evaluations to determine the perfect moment to harvest. They frequently sample grapes, measuring sugar levels

(Brix), acidity, and pH, while also tasting the fruit to assess flavor development.

Weather conditions play a significant role in determining harvest timing. In regions prone to rain during the harvest season, there is a risk of grape clusters absorbing excess water, which can dilute flavors and increase the likelihood of rot and disease. Conversely, a prolonged dry spell can concentrate sugars and flavors but may also lead to overripe grapes with high sugar levels and low acidity. Vineyard managers must constantly monitor weather forecasts and be prepared to adjust their harvest plans accordingly, sometimes opting to pick grapes earlier or later than initially planned to avoid adverse conditions.

Once the decision to harvest has been made, the next step is to choose the method of harvesting: manual or mechanical. Hand harvesting is labor-intensive but allows for greater precision and care. Workers carefully select and pick only the ripest clusters, often using small pruning shears to avoid damaging the vines. This method is particularly beneficial for high-quality wines, where the condition of the grapes is paramount. Hand harvesting also allows for the selection of individual berries, which is essential for certain styles of wine, such as late-harvest or botrytized wines, where only the most perfectly ripened or affected grapes are desired.

Mechanical harvesting, on the other hand, is much faster and more cost-effective, especially for large vineyards. Machines equipped with vibrating arms shake the grapevines, causing the ripe berries to fall off and be collected. While this method can be efficient, it may also result in a mix of ripe and unripe berries, leaves, and other debris. Advances in technology have improved the precision of mechanical harvesters, but they still cannot match the selectivity of human hands. Vineyard managers must weigh the benefits and drawbacks of each method, often using a combination of both depending on the specific needs of the vineyard and the type of wine being produced.

After the grapes are harvested, they must be transported to the winery as quickly and gently as possible to prevent oxidation and spoilage. The method of transportation varies based on the scale of the operation and the distance between the vineyard and the winery. For small, high-quality producers, grapes are often transported in small bins or crates to minimize damage. Larger producers may use trucks or trailers, which can hold greater quantities but require careful handling to avoid crushing the grapes.

Once at the winery, the grapes undergo an initial sorting process to remove any unwanted material, such as leaves, stems, or damaged fruit. This can be done by hand or with the aid of sorting tables and conveyor belts. The goal is to ensure that only the highest quality grapes proceed to the next stage of winemaking. Some wineries also use optical sorting machines, which employ cameras and sensors to identify and remove undesirable grapes with remarkable precision.

The next step in the harvest process is destemming and crushing. For most wines, the grapes are separated from their stems, which can impart bitter and astringent flavors if left in contact with the juice. This is typically done with a machine called a destemmer, which gently removes the stems while leaving the berries intact. The grapes are then lightly crushed to release their juice, a process that can be adjusted to achieve the desired level of extraction. For certain styles of wine, such as whole-cluster fermentation, the grapes are left with their stems, which can add complexity and structure to the wine.

Fermentation follows, where the grape juice is transformed into wine through the action of yeast. The specifics of this process vary widely depending on the type of wine being produced, but the quality of the grapes at harvest lays the foundation for the entire winemaking process. The careful timing and method of harvest ensure that the grapes possess the ideal balance of sugar, acidity, and flavor compounds, which will directly influence the character and quality of the finished wine.

In some cases, particularly for sparkling wines or certain white wines, grapes may undergo a process called cold stabilization before fermentation. This involves chilling the grape must (juice and solid parts) to precipitate out tartrates and other solids that could cause instability or haziness in the finished wine. This step is part of the meticulous care taken to ensure that the harvested grapes translate into a high-quality product.

The post-harvest period is also critical for the ongoing health of the vineyard. After the grapes are picked, the vines enter a phase of senescence, where they begin to store energy in their roots and trunks for the next growing season. Vineyard managers may take this time to apply fertilizers or soil amendments, based on soil tests conducted earlier in the year. They also prepare the vineyard for winter, ensuring that the vines are protected from potential frost damage and other environmental stresses.

Moreover, the end of the harvest season is an opportune moment for reflection and planning. Vineyard managers and winemakers review the outcomes of the year's harvest, assessing what worked well and what could be improved. They analyze data on yield, grape quality, and weather conditions to inform their strategies for the next growing season. This continuous cycle of assessment and adaptation is key to maintaining the health and productivity of the vineyard and ensuring the consistent production of high-quality grapes.

Chapter 3
Wine Production Process

From Grape to Juice

Transforming grapes into juice is a process steeped in tradition but refined with modern techniques. Each step, from selecting the grapes to extracting their essence, requires meticulous attention to detail. This journey from vine to glass is as much an art as it is a science, blending age-old practices with cutting-edge innovations to produce a product that reflects the vineyard's unique characteristics.

The journey begins in the vineyard, where the first crucial decision is the selection of grapes. The choice of grape variety is paramount, as different types yield distinct flavors and juice qualities. For instance, Concord grapes are known for their robust, sweet flavor, making them ideal for juice, while varieties like Muscadine offer a more aromatic profile. Once the variety is chosen, the condition of the grapes is the next consideration. Grapes must be at their peak ripeness, boasting the perfect balance of sweetness, acidity, and flavor.

Harvesting these grapes at the right time is critical. This timing is influenced by various factors, including the grape variety, the desired style of juice, and prevailing weather conditions. Vineyard managers rely on a mix of scientific measurements and sensory evaluations. They frequently test the grapes' sugar levels, acidity, and pH, all while tasting the fruit to gauge its flavor profile. This combination of data and experience guides the decision on when to pick the grapes, ensuring they are harvested at their optimal state.

Once harvested, the grapes need to be transported to the processing facility swiftly and gently to avoid bruising and oxidation. This is particularly important for juice production, where the freshness and integrity of the fruit directly impact the final product's quality. Smaller operations might use shallow bins to transport the grapes, minimizing the weight on each berry and reducing the risk of damage. Larger producers might employ more sophisticated methods, such as refrigerated trucks, to maintain the grapes' freshness over longer distances.

Upon arrival at the processing facility, the grapes undergo a meticulous sorting process. This step involves removing any leaves, stems, or damaged fruit that could negatively affect the juice's taste and clarity. Sorting can be done by hand for smaller batches or with the help of advanced sorting machines for larger quantities. The objective is to ensure that only the best grapes make it to the next stage.

The next step is destemming and crushing. Most juice producers prefer to remove the grape stems, as they can impart bitter and astringent flavors to the juice. This is typically done using a destemmer, which gently separates the stems from the berries. The grapes are then lightly crushed to break their skins and release the juice inside. This process must be carefully controlled to avoid over-crushing, which can release unwanted tannins and other compounds from the skins and seeds.

For white grape varieties, the crushed grapes, also known as must, are often pressed immediately to separate the juice from the skins, seeds, and pulp. This pressing process can be done using traditional basket presses or more modern bladder presses, which apply gentle pressure to extract the juice. The goal is to obtain clear, flavorful juice without extracting too many bitter or astringent compounds.

Red grape varieties, on the other hand, may undergo a period of maceration before pressing. During maceration, the crushed grapes are allowed to sit with their skins for a certain period, allowing the juice to extract color, flavor, and tannins from the skins. This step is crucial for producing red grape juice with a rich color and complex flavor profile. The duration of maceration can vary depending on the desired characteristics of the juice, ranging from a few hours to several days.

After pressing, the juice is collected and transferred to fermentation vessels if it is intended for further processing into wine. However, for grape juice, the next step is typically pasteurization. Pasteurization involves heating the juice to a specific temperature for a set period to kill any harmful bacteria and yeast that could cause spoilage. This step is crucial for ensuring the juice's safety and extending its shelf life. There are various methods of pasteurization, including batch pasteurization and flash pasteurization, each with its own advantages and challenges.

Once pasteurized, the juice is rapidly cooled to prevent any further microbial growth and to preserve its fresh flavor. It is then filtered to remove any remaining solids and to clarify the juice. The filtration process can range from simple straining through cheesecloth for small batches to more sophisticated filtration systems for larger quantities. The goal is to produce a clear, clean juice that is visually appealing and free of any unwanted particulates.

Packaging is the final step in the journey from grape to juice. The juice can be packaged in various containers, including glass bottles, plastic bottles, or aseptic cartons, depending on the producer's preferences and market demands. Each packaging method has its own set of benefits. Glass bottles are often chosen for their premium look and ability to preserve flavor without any risk of leaching chemicals. Plastic bottles offer convenience and durability, while aseptic cartons provide a long shelf life and are often more environmentally friendly.

Throughout the entire process, maintaining hygiene and temperature control is paramount. Any lapse in cleanliness can introduce spoilage organisms, compromising the quality and safety of the juice. Similarly, temperature fluctuations can affect the juice's flavor and stability. Producers must adhere to strict sanitation protocols and monitor temperatures closely at each stage.

The evolution of grape juice production has also seen the introduction of organic and biodynamic practices. These methods eschew synthetic chemicals and emphasize sustainability, both in the vineyard and the processing facility. For instance, organic grape juice production involves using organically grown grapes, free from pesticides and synthetic fertilizers. Biodynamic practices take this a step further, incorporating holistic and regenerative approaches to farming. These practices not only benefit the environment but also often result in juice with unique and vibrant flavors.

For beginners looking to make grape juice at home, the process can be simplified while still producing a delicious and wholesome product. Small-scale juice production involves similar steps: selecting ripe grapes, crushing them, pressing the juice, pasteurizing, and then bottling. Home producers can use household equipment like potato mashers for crushing and cheesecloth for straining, making the process accessible and enjoyable.

Fermentation Techniques

Fermentation is a transformative process that has been utilized for centuries to produce a variety of foods and beverages. At its core, fermentation involves the conversion of sugars into alcohol or acids by microorganisms such as yeast and bacteria. This process not only preserves food but also enhances its flavor, texture, and nutritional value. Understanding the intricacies of fermentation techniques is crucial for anyone looking to master the art of creating fermented products.

The journey of fermentation begins with the selection of raw materials. The quality of the starting ingredients directly impacts the final product. For instance, in wine fermentation, the choice of grape variety, its ripeness, and the conditions under which it was grown all play significant roles. In bread making, the type of flour and water quality are equally important. Fresh, high-quality ingredients provide the best starting point for a successful fermentation.

Once the raw materials are selected, the next step is to prepare them for fermentation. This preparation varies depending on the type of product being fermented. In winemaking, grapes are crushed to release their juice, which is then left to ferment. In bread making, flour and water are mixed to form dough, which is then allowed to rise. This initial preparation is crucial as it creates the environment in which the microorganisms can thrive.

The heart of the fermentation process lies in the choice and management of microorganisms. Different microorganisms produce different fermentation outcomes. Yeast, for instance, is responsible for alcoholic fermentation, converting sugars into alcohol and carbon dioxide. This is the process that transforms grape juice into wine and dough into bread. Bacteria, on the other hand, are responsible for lactic acid fermentation, which is used in the production of yogurt, sauerkraut, and sourdough bread. Selecting the right strain of yeast or bacteria is essential, as each strain contributes unique flavors and characteristics to the final product.

Temperature control is a critical aspect of fermentation. The rate at which fermentation occurs is highly dependent on temperature. For example, in winemaking, cooler temperatures (around 50-60°F) are often used for white wines to preserve delicate aromas, while warmer temperatures (70-85°F) are preferred for red wines to extract color and tannins. In bread making, dough is typically fermented at room temperature, but cooler temperatures can be used for a slower, more flavorful rise. Maintaining the appropriate temperature ensures that the fermentation proceeds at the desired rate and produces the intended flavors.

Oxygen management is another important factor. During the initial stages of fermentation, oxygen is often required by the yeast or bacteria to grow and multiply. However, once fermentation is underway, the presence of oxygen can be detrimental. For instance, in winemaking, exposure to oxygen can lead to oxidation, which can spoil the wine. Winemakers often use airlocks to allow carbon dioxide to escape while preventing oxygen from entering the fermentation vessel. Similarly, in bread making, dough is often covered to prevent it from drying out and to protect it from airborne contaminants.

Monitoring the progress of fermentation is essential to ensure a successful outcome. This involves regularly checking the temperature, pH, and other parameters. In winemaking, the sugar level is often measured using a hydrometer or refractometer to track the conversion of sugar to alcohol. In bread making, the dough's rise and texture are indicators of fermentation progress. Keeping a close eye on these parameters allows for timely adjustments to be made if necessary.

Once fermentation is complete, the next step is to process the fermented product. In winemaking, this involves pressing the fermented grape must to separate the wine from the skins and seeds, followed by aging and bottling. In bread making, the fermented dough is shaped and baked. Proper handling at this stage is crucial to preserving the flavors and qualities developed during fermentation.

Sanitation is a key aspect of successful fermentation. Contamination by unwanted microorganisms can spoil the product and pose health risks. This is why it is important to maintain a clean working environment and sanitize all equipment and utensils before use. In commercial settings, stringent sanitation protocols are followed to ensure the safety and quality of the final product.

The science of fermentation has advanced significantly, providing a deeper understanding of the microorganisms involved and the conditions that favor their activity. This knowledge allows for greater control over the fermentation process, resulting in consistent and high-quality products. For example, the development of pure yeast cultures has revolutionized winemaking and brewing, allowing for the production of wines and beers with specific desired characteristics.

However, traditional fermentation techniques that rely on wild or natural fermentation are still widely practiced and valued for the unique flavors they produce. In natural wine making, for instance, wild yeasts present on the grape skins initiate fermentation, resulting in wines with complex and varied flavor profiles. Similarly, in sourdough bread making, wild yeast and lactic acid bacteria from the environment are used to leaven the bread, producing a distinctive tangy flavor.

Fermentation is not limited to food and beverages. It also plays a crucial role in the production of biofuels, pharmaceuticals, and other industrial products. The principles of fermentation remain the same, but the scale and specific techniques may vary. For example, in biofuel production, large fermenters are used to convert biomass into ethanol, while in pharmaceutical production, fermentation is used to produce antibiotics and other drugs.

For beginners looking to explore fermentation at home, starting with simple projects like making yogurt, sauerkraut, or sourdough bread can be a rewarding experience. These projects require minimal equipment and ingredients, yet provide a hands-on understanding of the fermentation process. As confidence and experience grow, more complex projects like brewing beer or making wine can be undertaken.

Aging and Maturation

Aging and maturation are pivotal processes in the development of many fermented and distilled products, transforming them from raw, sometimes harsh, beginnings into complex, refined masterpieces. These stages are where the magic truly happens, where flavors meld, textures evolve, and the essence of the product fully blossoms. Understanding the intricacies of aging and maturation is essential for anyone looking to master the craft of producing exceptional beverages and foods.

The journey of aging begins right after fermentation or distillation. For alcoholic beverages like wine, beer, and spirits, the aging process can significantly alter the flavor profile, aroma, and mouthfeel. The vessel in which the product is aged plays a crucial role. Oak barrels, for instance, are renowned for the unique characteristics they impart. The type of oak, its origin, and whether it's new or previously used all influence the final product. New oak barrels contribute flavors like vanilla, spice, and caramel, while used barrels add subtle complexity without overpowering the original flavors.

In winemaking, barrel aging is an art form. Red wines often benefit from extended aging in oak barrels, which allows tannins to soften and flavors to integrate. This process can take anywhere from a few months to several years, depending on the desired outcome. White wines, on the other hand, may be aged in stainless steel tanks to preserve their fresh, fruity characteristics, or in oak barrels to add richness and depth. Monitoring the wine's progress during aging is crucial, as it must be racked periodically to remove sediment and prevent spoilage.

Beer, particularly styles like stouts, porters, and strong ales, can also undergo aging. Barrel-aging beer introduces complex flavors from the wood and any residual spirits or wines that previously occupied the barrel. This can result in a beer with layers of flavors, such as bourbon, sherry, or even hints of sourness from wild yeast strains. The aging period for beer is typically shorter than for wine, ranging from a few months to a year, but the impact on flavor can be profound.

Spirits like whiskey, rum, and brandy undergo a transformative aging process in wooden casks. The interaction between the spirit and the wood, along with environmental factors such as temperature and humidity, plays a significant role in developing the spirit's character. In warm climates, spirits age faster due to increased interaction with the wood, while cooler climates result in a slower, more gradual maturation. This is why scotch whisky, aged in the cool, damp climate of Scotland, develops a different profile compared to bourbon, aged in the warmer conditions of Kentucky.

Cheese maturation, or affinage, is another fascinating aspect of aging. After the initial production, cheeses are aged in specific conditions to develop their flavor, texture, and rind. The environment, including temperature, humidity, and airflow, is meticulously controlled to encourage the growth of beneficial molds and bacteria. For example, blue cheeses like Roquefort are aged in caves with high humidity, which promotes the development of blue mold veins. Hard cheeses like Parmesan are aged in cool, dry conditions, leading to a firm texture and concentrated flavor.

Cured meats also benefit immensely from aging. Products like prosciutto, salami, and chorizo undergo a drying and maturation process where their flavors intensify and textures firm up. The key to successful meat aging is maintaining the right balance of temperature and humidity to prevent spoilage while allowing the natural enzymes to break down proteins and fats, enhancing the meat's flavor and tenderness.

The maturation of fermentative foods like sauerkraut, kimchi, and miso is equally important. These products undergo a period of fermentation followed by aging, during which their flavors deepen and complex layers develop. Kimchi, for example, can be enjoyed fresh for its crunchy texture and bright flavors, or aged for a more robust, tangy profile. Miso, a fermented soybean paste, is aged for varying lengths of time, from a few months for a light, sweet miso to several years for a dark, intense miso.

Controlling the environment during aging and maturation is paramount. Temperature and humidity must be carefully regulated to ensure the right conditions for each product. For cheese and meats, this often means using specialized aging rooms or caves with precise climate control. For beverages, it may involve selecting the right storage facilities, such as cellars for wine or warehouses for spirits, each designed to maintain optimal aging conditions.

Time is the ultimate factor in aging and maturation. Patience is required, as rushing the process can lead to subpar results. The adage "good things come to those who wait" holds true in the world of fermented and distilled products. Each product has its own timeline, and understanding when it has reached its peak is an essential skill. This often involves sensory evaluation—tasting and smelling the product at various stages to determine its progress and readiness.

Blending is another crucial aspect of maturation, particularly in the production of spirits and wine. Master blenders or winemakers often combine products from different barrels or batches to achieve a consistent and balanced final product. This requires a deep understanding of how different components interact and complement each other. For instance, in whiskey production, blending older, more mature whiskies with younger spirits can create a balanced profile that showcases the best attributes of both.

Aging and maturation are not without risks. Spoilage, oxidation, and contamination are constant threats. Ensuring cleanliness and proper handling throughout the process is essential to mitigate these risks. For example, wine barrels must be kept clean and sulfured to prevent microbial growth, and cheese must be regularly inspected for undesirable molds.

Bottling and Storage

Bottling and storage are the final, crucial steps in the production process that ensure your hard work and dedication result in a high-quality finished product. Whether you're dealing with wine, beer, spirits, or fermented foods, these stages can make or break the end result. Proper techniques and careful attention to detail during bottling and storage can preserve the flavors, aromas, and overall quality of your creation.

When it comes to bottling, preparation is key. Before you begin, ensure that all equipment, including bottles, caps, corks, and any other tools, are thoroughly cleaned and sanitized. Contamination at this stage can spoil your product, rendering your efforts futile. Use a sanitizing solution that is food-safe and effective, and allow everything to air dry completely.

For wine, the type of bottle and closure you choose can have a significant impact on the aging process and overall quality. Traditional wine bottles come in various shapes and colors, each suited to different types of wine. Dark-colored bottles are typically used for red wines as they protect the wine from light exposure, which can lead to oxidation. Clear bottles are often used for white and rosé wines, where light exposure is less of a concern. Cork closures are traditional for wines meant to age and evolve over time, allowing a small amount of oxygen to interact with the wine. Screw caps, on the other hand, are great for wines intended to be consumed young, as they provide a tight seal and prevent oxidation.

In beer production, bottling is an art in itself. Many homebrewers and craft breweries opt for glass bottles, which do an excellent job of preserving the beer's carbonation and flavor. Brown glass is preferred because it blocks harmful UV rays that can cause skunky off-flavors. When bottling beer, it's vital to ensure that the beer is carbonated to the desired level. This is often achieved through bottle conditioning, where a small amount of sugar is added to the beer before sealing it. The residual yeast ferments the sugar, producing carbon dioxide and naturally carbonating the beer. Caps should be crimped tightly to prevent any gas from escaping.

For spirits, bottling involves less concern about oxidation and carbonation but still requires precision. Glass bottles are the standard for spirits, as they do not interact with the liquid and preserve its integrity. The shape and design of the bottle can also add to the aesthetic appeal and brand identity of the spirit. Sealing spirits with a tight-fitting cork or screw cap ensures that no air can enter and affect the spirit's quality. Some high-end spirits use wax seals for an added layer of protection and a touch of elegance.

Fermented foods like sauerkraut, kimchi, and pickles are typically stored in jars. Choosing the right jar is essential to maintain the product's quality and safety. Glass jars with airtight lids are ideal, as they prevent contamination and preserve the ferment's flavors and textures. Before filling the jars, ensure they are sterilized to avoid introducing any unwanted bacteria. Once filled, the jars should be sealed tightly and stored in a cool, dark place to continue the fermentation process at a controlled rate.

Storage conditions can significantly impact the longevity and quality of your bottled products. Temperature, light, and humidity are the three critical factors to consider. For wine, a consistent storage temperature of around 55°F (13°C) is ideal, with a humidity level of about 70%. These conditions help prevent the cork from drying out and allow the wine to age gracefully. Wine should be stored on its side to keep the cork moist, which helps maintain a good seal and prevents oxidation.

Beer storage is somewhat similar, with a cool, dark environment being optimal. Temperatures of around 50-55°F (10-13°C) are generally recommended for most beers, though some styles, like lagers, benefit from colder storage. Light exposure can cause beer to develop off-flavors, so keeping beer in a dark place is essential. Store beer bottles upright to minimize the surface area exposed to oxygen and reduce the risk of oxidation.

Spirits are more robust and less sensitive to storage conditions, but they still benefit from being kept in a cool, dark place. Avoid storing spirits in areas with fluctuating temperatures, as this can cause the liquid to expand and contract, potentially compromising the seal and leading to evaporation. While spirits do not age in the bottle as wine does, proper storage ensures they retain their quality over time.

For fermented foods, a cool environment slows down the fermentation process and prolongs the shelf life. Refrigeration is often the best option, especially once the desired level of fermentation is achieved. Keeping jars in the fridge not only preserves the texture and flavor but also ensures the product remains safe to consume.

Labeling is another critical aspect of bottling and storage. Accurate labels provide essential information about the product, such as the type, date of bottling, alcohol content (for beverages), and any other relevant details. For wines and beers, labels can also include tasting notes, suggested serving temperatures, and pairing recommendations. Proper labeling helps in tracking the age and condition of the product, making it easier to manage your inventory and enjoy the products at their peak.

One often overlooked aspect of bottling and storage is the potential for bottle shock. This phenomenon occurs when wine or beer is disturbed during bottling, causing the flavors to become muted or disjointed. Allowing the bottles to rest for a few weeks after bottling can help them recover and integrate, ensuring the final product is as intended.

Sustainable Winemaking Practices

Sustainable winemaking practices have become increasingly important in the modern wine industry, not only for their environmental benefits but also for their potential to enhance wine quality and ensure the long-term viability of vineyards. Embracing sustainability involves a holistic approach that considers the environmental, social, and economic impacts of winemaking. It requires a commitment to reducing waste, conserving natural resources, and promoting biodiversity, all while maintaining or improving the quality of the wine produced.

One of the core principles of sustainable winemaking is the responsible management of the vineyard. This starts with the soil, which is the foundation of any healthy vineyard. Sustainable viticulture practices focus on maintaining soil health through methods such as cover cropping, composting, and minimal tillage. Cover crops, like legumes and grasses, are planted between vine rows to prevent soil erosion, enhance soil fertility, and promote biodiversity. These plants can fix nitrogen, improve soil structure, and provide habitat for beneficial insects.

Water management is another critical aspect of sustainable viticulture. With climate change causing more frequent and severe droughts in many wine-growing regions, efficient water use is essential. Drip irrigation systems, which deliver water directly to the root zone of each vine, can significantly reduce water waste compared to traditional flood or sprinkler irrigation. Additionally, some vineyards implement dry farming techniques, relying solely on natural rainfall to irrigate the vines. This not only conserves water but can also produce grapes with more concentrated flavors.

Pest management is a significant challenge in viticulture, but sustainable practices aim to reduce reliance on chemical pesticides. Integrated Pest Management (IPM) is a holistic approach that combines biological, cultural, and mechanical methods to control pests. This includes encouraging natural predators, such as birds and beneficial insects, to keep pest populations in check. Vineyards may also use pheromone traps or barriers to disrupt pest mating cycles. By reducing chemical inputs,

IPM helps protect the environment, vineyard workers, and consumers.

Energy efficiency is another crucial component of sustainable winemaking. Wineries consume substantial amounts of energy for heating, cooling, and operating equipment. Many sustainable wineries invest in renewable energy sources, such as solar panels or wind turbines, to reduce their carbon footprint. Energy-efficient lighting, insulation, and equipment can also lower energy consumption. Some wineries even harness geothermal energy for heating and cooling, taking advantage of the earth's natural temperature regulation.

Waste management in sustainable wineries focuses on reducing, reusing, and recycling. Grape pomace, the solid remains of grapes after pressing, can be composted and returned to the vineyard as a natural fertilizer. It can also be used to produce products like grape seed oil or animal feed. Water used in the winemaking process is often treated and recycled for irrigation or cleaning. Many wineries have also moved towards using lightweight, recyclable packaging materials to minimize their environmental impact.

Sustainable winemaking practices extend to the social and economic aspects of the business. Fair labor practices, community engagement, and support for local economies are all integral to a truly sustainable winery. This might involve paying fair wages, providing safe working conditions, and offering training and development opportunities for employees. Engaging with local communities through educational programs, events, and collaborations can foster positive relationships and support for the winery.

Biodiversity is another vital element of sustainable viticulture. Maintaining a diverse ecosystem within and around the vineyard can enhance resilience to pests and diseases, improve soil health, and support a range of wildlife. This can be achieved by preserving natural habitats, planting native vegetation, and creating wildlife corridors. Some vineyards even incorporate livestock, such as sheep or chickens, to control weeds and pests naturally while adding to the farm's biodiversity.

Sustainable winemaking also involves careful consideration of the chemicals used in the vineyard and winery. Organic and biodynamic farming practices, which eschew synthetic chemicals in favor of natural alternatives, are increasingly popular. Organic farming focuses on building healthy soils and ecosystems, using compost, green manure, and natural pest control methods. Biodynamic farming takes this a step further by incorporating holistic and spiritual principles, such as planting according to lunar cycles and using special preparations to enhance soil and plant health.

Certification programs can help wineries demonstrate their commitment to sustainability. Certifications such as the Sustainable Winegrowing Certification, Organic Certification, and Biodynamic Certification provide guidelines and standards for sustainable practices. Achieving certification can enhance a winery's reputation, appeal to environmentally conscious consumers, and sometimes even command higher prices for their wines.

The benefits of sustainable winemaking practices extend beyond environmental stewardship. Wines produced sustainably often have a unique sense of place, reflecting the terroir and the care taken in their production. Consumers are increasingly seeking out wines that align with their values, and sustainable practices can help wineries differentiate themselves in a competitive market. Additionally, sustainable practices can improve the long-term health and productivity of the vineyard, ensuring that it can continue to produce high-quality grapes for generations to come.

Innovation and technology play significant roles in advancing sustainable winemaking. Precision viticulture, which uses GPS, sensors, and data analytics, allows for more targeted and efficient vineyard management. For example, sensors can monitor soil moisture levels, helping to optimize irrigation and reduce water use. Drones can be used to assess vine health and identify areas of stress or disease. These technologies enable more precise and sustainable management of vineyard resources.

Education and collaboration are essential for the continued advancement of sustainable practices in the wine industry. Organizations such as the California Sustainable Winegrowing Alliance and the International Wineries for Climate Action provide resources, training, and support for wineries looking to adopt sustainable practices. Sharing knowledge and experiences within the industry can drive innovation and improve sustainability across the board.

Chapter 4

Types of Wine

Red Wines

Red wines have captivated wine enthusiasts for centuries, offering a rich tapestry of flavors, aromas, and textures that can vary dramatically depending on the grape variety, region, and winemaking techniques employed. The journey from vineyard to bottle is an intricate dance of science and art, where every decision made by the winemaker influences the final product. Understanding red wines involves delving into the characteristics of key grape varieties, the terroir, the winemaking process, and the best practices for enjoying these robust beverages.

Cabernet Sauvignon is often hailed as the king of red wines, known for its full body, bold tannins, and complex flavor profile. Originating from the Bordeaux region of France, this grape variety has found a second home in California's Napa Valley, where it thrives in the warm, sunny climate. The flavors of Cabernet Sauvignon can range from dark fruits like blackcurrant and blackberry to more savory notes of green bell pepper, mint, and cigar box, especially when aged in oak. The high tannin content provides structure and aging potential, allowing the wine to develop and evolve over time.

Merlot, another Bordeaux native, offers a softer, more approachable profile compared to Cabernet Sauvignon. It is often used in blends to add suppleness and fruitiness, but it also shines as a single varietal wine. Merlot is characterized by its medium to full body, velvety texture, and flavors of plum, black cherry, and chocolate. It can be enjoyed young but also has the potential to age gracefully, developing additional complexity and depth.

Pinot Noir stands in stark contrast to the robust nature of Cabernet Sauvignon and Merlot. Known for its elegance and finesse, Pinot Noir is a delicate grape that thrives in cooler climates such as Burgundy in France and Oregon in the United States. This thin-skinned grape produces light to medium-bodied wines with a silky texture and flavors that can range from red fruits like cherry and raspberry to earthy notes of mushroom and forest floor. Pinot Noir's subtlety and complexity make it a favorite among connoisseurs and a versatile pairing for a wide range of foods.

Syrah, or Shiraz as it is known in Australia, is a grape that produces wines with intense flavors and a rich, full-bodied profile. The Northern Rhône region of France is renowned for its Syrah wines, which often exhibit flavors of blackberry, plum, and black pepper, along with floral and smoky notes. In contrast, Australian Shiraz tends to be more fruit-forward, with jammy berry flavors and a hint of spice. Syrah's robust nature and high tannin content make it a great candidate for aging, allowing the wine to develop additional layers of complexity over time.

Zinfandel, a grape with a somewhat mysterious origin, is now primarily associated with California. Known for its bold fruit flavors and high alcohol content, Zinfandel can produce a wide range of styles, from light and fruity to rich and jammy. Flavors of raspberry, blackberry, and black pepper are common, and the wine's spicy character makes it a popular choice for pairing with barbecued meats and spicy dishes.

Malbec, originally from France but now most famously grown in Argentina, offers a unique combination of dark fruit flavors, robust tannins, and a smooth finish. Argentine Malbecs are known for their deep color, flavors of blackberry, plum, and chocolate, and a touch of smokiness. The high altitude vineyards of Argentina provide the perfect conditions for growing Malbec, resulting in wines that are both powerful and elegant.

The terroir, or the unique combination of soil, climate, and geography, plays a crucial role in shaping the character of red wines. For example, the volcanic soils of Mount Etna in Sicily impart a distinct minerality to the Nerello Mascalese wines produced there, while the limestone-rich soils of Bordeaux contribute to the structure and complexity of its famous red blends. Winemakers often speak of a wine's sense of place, or terroir, as a defining characteristic that sets it apart from others.

The winemaking process for red wines involves several key steps, each of which can influence the final product. After harvesting, the grapes are typically destemmed and crushed, releasing the juice and starting the fermentation process. During fermentation, the grape skins remain in contact with the juice, imparting color, tannins, and flavors to the wine. This process, known as maceration, can vary in duration depending on the desired style of wine. A longer maceration period can result in a wine with more intense color and tannins, while a shorter maceration period can produce a lighter, more delicate wine.

Once fermentation is complete, the wine is often aged in oak barrels, which can add additional flavors and complexity. The type of oak, the age of the barrels, and the length of time the wine spends in oak can all influence the final product. New oak barrels tend to impart more pronounced flavors of vanilla, spice, and toast, while older barrels contribute more subtle nuances. Some red wines, particularly those intended for early consumption, may be aged in stainless steel or concrete tanks to preserve their fresh fruit character.

Blending is another important aspect of red winemaking. Many of the world's most famous red wines, such as Bordeaux blends, are the result of combining different grape varieties to achieve a harmonious balance of flavors, aromas, and textures. Blending allows winemakers to enhance the complexity and depth of a wine, creating a final product that is greater than the sum of its parts.

Enjoying red wine at its best involves a few considerations. Serving temperature is crucial; overly warm red wine can taste flat and overly alcoholic, while too cold a temperature can mute its flavors. Generally, full-bodied reds like Cabernet Sauvignon and Syrah are best served slightly below room temperature, around 60-65°F (15-18°C), while lighter reds like Pinot Noir can be enjoyed a bit cooler, around 55-60°F (13-15°C).

Decanting can also enhance the enjoyment of red wine, particularly for younger, tannic wines. Decanting involves pouring the wine into a separate vessel to aerate it and allow it to breathe, which can help soften tannins and release aromas. Older wines, which may have sediment, can also benefit from decanting to separate the clear wine from the sediment.

Red wines are incredibly versatile when it comes to food pairings. The robust flavors and tannins of Cabernet Sauvignon make it an excellent match for hearty dishes like steak, lamb, and rich stews. Merlot's softer profile pairs well with roasted poultry, pork, and dishes with tomato-based sauces. Pinot Noir's bright acidity and subtlety make it a great choice for lighter fare such as salmon, duck, and mushroom dishes. Syrah's bold flavors and spice can stand up to grilled meats, sausages, and spicy foods, while Zinfandel's fruit-forward character pairs well with barbecued ribs, burgers, and pizza. Malbec's rich, dark fruit flavors and smooth finish make it a perfect match for grilled or roasted meats, especially beef.

White Wines

White wines are a world unto themselves, presenting a spectrum of flavors, aromas, and textures that can delight and surprise even the most seasoned wine enthusiasts. Unlike their red counterparts, white wines are generally made from green-skinned grapes, with the juice often fermented without the grape skins, resulting in a lighter color and body. The diversity of white wines is vast, from the crisp and refreshing to the rich and full-bodied, each offering unique experiences based on grape variety, region, and winemaking techniques.

Chardonnay is one of the most well-known and versatile white wine grapes, originating from the Burgundy region of France. It can produce a wide range of styles, from steely and mineral-driven wines to rich, buttery, and oak-aged versions. In cooler climates like Chablis, Chardonnay tends to exhibit high acidity and flavors of green apple, lemon, and flint. Conversely, in warmer regions such as California and Australia, it often showcases ripe tropical fruit flavors, along with hints of vanilla and spice from oak aging. This adaptability makes Chardonnay a favorite among winemakers and consumers alike, capable of complementing a variety of dishes from seafood to poultry and creamy pasta.

Sauvignon Blanc, hailing from the Loire Valley in France and now widely planted in New Zealand, California, and South Africa, is celebrated for its vibrant acidity and distinctive aromatic profile. Typical flavors include green apple, lime, and passion fruit, often accompanied by herbaceous notes like bell pepper and freshly cut grass. In regions like Sancerre and Pouilly-Fumé, Sauvignon Blancs are often more restrained, with flinty minerality and a crisp, clean finish. New Zealand versions, particularly from Marlborough, tend to be more exuberant, bursting with tropical fruit flavors and a zesty edge. This grape's refreshing nature makes it an excellent match for salads, goat cheese, seafood, and dishes with herbal components.

Riesling is another versatile white grape, known for its high acidity and ability to produce wines across a spectrum of sweetness levels, from bone-dry to lusciously sweet. Originating in Germany's Rhine region, Riesling grapes thrive in cool climates, developing complex flavors of green apple, peach, and apricot, often with a distinctive petrol note as they age. German Rieslings are renowned for their balance of sweetness and acidity, making them perfect for pairing with spicy cuisine, particularly dishes from Asian and Indian traditions. Dry Rieslings from Alsace in France or Clare Valley in Australia are equally compelling, offering a crisp, mineral-driven profile that complements seafood, pork, and poultry.

Pinot Grigio, also known as Pinot Gris, offers yet another dimension to white wines. In Italy, where it is most commonly referred to as Pinot Grigio, the wines are typically light-bodied with high acidity and flavors of citrus, green apple, and pear. These wines are often straightforward and easy-drinking, making them popular for casual sipping and pairing with light dishes like salads, seafood, and light pasta dishes. In contrast, the Alsace region of France produces Pinot Gris in a richer, more full-bodied style, with flavors of ripe pear, apple, and honey, often accompanied by a slightly oily texture. These wines can handle more robust pairings, such as roasted poultry, pork, and dishes with creamy sauces.

Chenin Blanc, a grape with a long history in France's Loire Valley, is incredibly versatile, capable of producing a wide array of wine styles from dry to sweet, still to sparkling. In the Loire, Vouvray wines showcase Chenin Blanc's potential for both dry and sweet styles, often with flavors of apple, quince, and honey, and a vibrant acidity that allows these wines to age gracefully. South Africa has also embraced Chenin Blanc, producing wines that range from fresh and fruity to rich and oaky, often with a distinctive tropical fruit character. The grape's versatility makes it suitable for pairing with a broad range of foods, from seafood and salads to richer dishes like pork and veal.

Gewürztraminer is known for its aromatic intensity and exotic flavors, making it a standout among white wines. Originating from the Alsace region of France, this grape produces wines with a distinctive lychee, rose petal, and spice profile, often with a slightly oily texture and a touch of sweetness. The heady aromas and bold flavors of Gewürztraminer make it an excellent match for spicy cuisine, particularly dishes from Thai and Indian traditions, as well as strong cheeses and rich, savory dishes.

The terroir, or the unique combination of soil, climate, and geography, significantly influences the character of white wines. For instance, the limestone-rich soils of Chablis contribute to the high acidity and mineral notes in its Chardonnay, while the volcanic soils of Mount Etna in Sicily impart a distinct minerality to its Carricante wines. In the Mosel region of Germany, the steep slate slopes help retain heat, promoting the ripening of Riesling grapes and imparting a characteristic flinty minerality to the wines. Terroir is a crucial element that gives each wine its unique sense of place, or "gout de terroir," making it a fascinating aspect for wine enthusiasts to explore.

The winemaking process for white wines involves several key steps that influence the final product. After harvesting, white grapes are typically pressed immediately to separate the juice from the skins, minimizing tannin extraction and color. The juice is then clarified and fermented, often at cooler temperatures than red wines, to preserve the fresh, fruity aromas. Fermentation vessels can vary, with stainless steel tanks being common for their ability to maintain a clean, pure expression of the grape. Oak barrels may be used for fermentation and aging to add complexity, richness, and flavors like vanilla, toast, and spice.

Malolactic fermentation, a secondary process where lactic acid bacteria convert malic acid to the softer lactic acid, can be used to soften the acidity and add a creamy texture, particularly in Chardonnay. Lees aging, where the wine remains in contact with dead yeast cells, can also add a creamy texture and enhance the flavor complexity, often imparting notes of bread dough, nuts, and butter.

Enjoying white wine at its best involves a few practical considerations. Serving temperature is important, with most white wines best enjoyed chilled but not too cold, as excessive cold can mute the aromas and flavors. Light-bodied whites like Sauvignon Blanc and Pinot Grigio are typically served around 45-50°F (7-10°C), while fuller-bodied whites like Chardonnay and Viognier are best served slightly warmer, around 50-55°F (10-13°C).

Glassware also plays a role in the enjoyment of white wine. A smaller, narrower glass is often recommended for light-bodied whites to concentrate the delicate aromas, while a larger bowl is suitable for fuller-bodied whites to allow the wine to breathe and release more complex aromas. Swirling the wine in the glass can enhance the olfactory experience, allowing the aromas to open up and providing a preview of the flavors to come.

Pairing white wine with food can elevate both the wine and the dish, creating a harmonious dining experience. The high acidity and fresh fruit flavors of Sauvignon Blanc make it a great match for goat cheese, salads, and seafood, while the rich, buttery profile of oaked Chardonnay complements dishes with cream sauces, lobster, and roasted poultry. The sweetness and acidity of Riesling can balance the heat of spicy dishes, making it a perfect partner for Asian cuisine. Light, crisp Pinot Grigio pairs well with antipasti, seafood, and light pasta dishes, while the aromatic intensity of Gewürztraminer can stand up to strong cheeses, spicy dishes, and rich, savory foods.

Rosé Wines

Rosé wines, with their alluring pink hues and refreshing profiles, have captivated wine enthusiasts around the world. They straddle the line between red and white wines, offering a unique tasting experience that combines the best of both worlds. The production of rosé wines is an art that involves specific techniques to achieve their distinctive color and flavor, making them a fascinating subject for both novice and seasoned wine lovers.

The journey of a rosé wine begins in the vineyard, where the choice of grape varieties plays a crucial role. While many red grape varieties can be used to produce rosé, some of the most common include Grenache, Syrah, Mourvèdre, Pinot Noir, and Sangiovese. Each grape variety brings its own set of characteristics to the wine, influencing the flavor profile, color, and aroma. The terroir, or the unique combination of soil, climate, and geography, also significantly impacts the final product. For instance, the sun-drenched vineyards of Provence in southern France are renowned for producing some of the world's most celebrated rosé wines, characterized by their pale color and delicate flavors.

The production of rosé wine typically involves one of three methods: direct pressing, maceration, or the saignée method. Direct pressing, often used in Provence, involves gently pressing red grapes to extract juice with minimal skin contact, resulting in a very pale pink color. This method produces rosés that are light and crisp, with subtle flavors and aromas. Maceration, on the other hand, allows the grape skins to remain in contact with the juice for a longer period, usually a few hours to a couple of days, before fermentation. This technique results in a deeper color and more intense flavor profile, often with notes of red berries and floral aromas. The saignée method, which translates to "bleeding," involves siphoning off a portion of the juice from a red wine fermentation, concentrating the red wine and producing a byproduct that is vinified separately into rosé. This method often results in a rosé with a richer color and more robust flavors.

Rosé wines can range in style from bone-dry to sweet, with a variety of flavors and aromas that appeal to a wide audience. Dry rosés, which are the most common, typically exhibit bright acidity and flavors of red fruit such as strawberry, raspberry, and cherry, often accompanied by floral and citrus notes. These wines are incredibly versatile and pair well with a variety of foods, making them a popular choice for summer picnics, barbecues, and alfresco dining. Sweet rosés, on the other hand, tend to have lower acidity and more pronounced fruit flavors, often with a hint of residual sugar that adds a touch of sweetness. These wines can be enjoyed on their own as a refreshing aperitif or paired with desserts and spicy dishes.

One of the most renowned regions for rosé wine production is Provence, where the tradition of rosé winemaking dates back thousands of years. The rosés of Provence are typically pale in color, with delicate flavors of red berries, citrus, and herbs. The region's Mediterranean climate, with its warm days and cool nights, allows the grapes to ripen fully while retaining their natural acidity. The soils, which are a mix of limestone, clay, and schist, also contribute to the unique character of Provence rosés, adding minerality and complexity to the wines. These wines are often enjoyed young, within a year or two of the vintage, to preserve their fresh and vibrant qualities.

Other notable regions for rosé production include Tavel in the Rhône Valley, where the rosés are known for their deep color and full-bodied structure, and the Loire Valley, which produces a range of styles from dry to sweet. In Spain, the Navarra region is famous for its rosados, made primarily from Garnacha (Grenache) grapes, while Italy's Veneto region produces a popular sparkling rosé called Prosecco Rosé. Each of these regions brings its own unique approach to rosé winemaking, resulting in a diverse array of styles and flavors for wine lovers to explore.

The versatility of rosé wine extends beyond its flavor profile and food pairings. Rosé has become a symbol of summer and outdoor gatherings, with its refreshing character making it the perfect choice for warm-weather sipping. Its popularity has surged in recent years, driven in part by a growing appreciation for its quality and complexity. No longer seen as merely a byproduct or a simple, sweet wine, rosé has earned its place alongside red and white wines as a serious and sophisticated option.

Serving rosé wine at the right temperature is crucial to fully appreciating its nuances. Generally, rosé should be served chilled, but not too cold, as excessive cold can mute the delicate aromas and flavors. A temperature range of 45-55°F (7-13°C) is ideal, with lighter, crisper rosés on the cooler end and fuller-bodied, more complex rosés slightly warmer. The choice of glassware can also enhance the drinking experience. A tulip-shaped white wine glass is often recommended, as it allows the aromas to concentrate and the wine to breathe.

Pairing rosé wine with food can elevate both the wine and the dish, creating a harmonious dining experience. The bright acidity and fruit-forward nature of dry rosés make them an excellent match for a wide range of foods. They pair particularly well with Mediterranean cuisine, including dishes like grilled vegetables, seafood, and salads. The herbal and citrus notes in Provence rosés complement the flavors of fresh herbs, olive oil, and garlic commonly found in these dishes. Fuller-bodied rosés, such as those from Tavel, can stand up to heartier fare like grilled meats, sausages, and rich sauces. Sweet rosés, with their touch of residual sugar, are a great choice for spicy foods, as the sweetness can balance the heat and enhance the overall flavor experience. They also pair well with fruit-based desserts, such as strawberry shortcake or peach cobbler, adding a refreshing counterpoint to the sweetness of the dish.

The rise of rosé wine has also led to a boom in rosé tourism, with many wine regions offering tours and tastings specifically focused on rosé. Provence, in particular, has become a popular destination for rosé enthusiasts, with its picturesque vineyards, charming villages, and stunning coastal scenery. Visitors can explore the region's wineries, learn about the history and production of rosé, and enjoy tastings of some of the world's finest examples. Other regions, such as the Napa Valley in California and the Navarra region in Spain, also offer rosé-focused experiences, allowing wine lovers to immerse themselves in the world of rosé.

As the popularity of rosé continues to grow, winemakers are experimenting with new techniques and styles to push the boundaries of what rosé can be. From sparkling rosés to barrel-aged versions, there is a growing diversity in the world of rosé wine, offering something for every palate and occasion. This innovation and creativity are helping to elevate the status of rosé and ensure its place as a beloved and respected category of wine.

Sparkling Wines

Sparkling wines, known for their effervescent charm and celebratory aura, hold a special place in the world of winemaking. These wines, with their lively bubbles and vibrant flavors, have been associated with joy and festivity for centuries. The allure of sparkling wines lies not only in their taste but also in the meticulous process of their creation, which transforms ordinary grapes into extraordinary elixirs.

The journey of a sparkling wine begins in the vineyard, where the selection of grape varieties is crucial. Common grapes used in sparkling wine production include Chardonnay, Pinot Noir, and Pinot Meunier, especially in the renowned Champagne region of France. However, other regions employ different varieties, such as Prosecco's Glera grape in Italy or Spain's Macabeo, Parellada, and Xarel-lo trio in Cava. The choice of grapes significantly influences the wine's flavor profile, acidity, and aging potential.

The production of sparkling wine involves several methods, each imparting unique characteristics to the final product. The most prestigious and labor-intensive method is the Traditional Method, or Méthode Champenoise, famously used in Champagne. This process begins with the primary fermentation, where still wine is created. The wine is then bottled with a mixture of sugar and yeast, initiating a second fermentation within the bottle. This fermentation produces carbon dioxide, which is trapped in the wine, creating the signature bubbles. The bottles are aged on their lees (dead yeast cells) for a period ranging from several months to several years, contributing to the wine's complexity and creamy texture. After aging, the bottles undergo riddling, where they are gradually tilted and rotated to collect the lees in the neck of the bottle. The lees are then removed through a process called disgorging, and the wine is topped up with a mixture of wine and sugar, known as dosage, to balance its acidity and sweetness.

Another popular method is the Charmat Method, or Tank Method, used primarily for producing Prosecco and other affordable sparkling wines. In this method, the second fermentation occurs in large pressurized tanks rather than individual bottles. The wine is then filtered and bottled under pressure. This approach is faster and less expensive than the Traditional Method, resulting in wines that are typically fresher and fruitier, with larger, more exuberant bubbles.

The Transfer Method combines elements of both the Traditional and Charmat methods. The wine undergoes secondary fermentation in the bottle, similar to the Traditional Method, but is then transferred to a pressurized tank for filtration and dosage before being re-bottled. This method retains some of the complexity of bottle fermentation while allowing for more efficient production.

Sparkling wines can vary greatly in style, from dry to sweet, and can be white, rosé, or even red. The sweetness level of sparkling wine is indicated by terms such as Brut, Extra Dry, Sec, and Demi-Sec. Brut, the driest style, contains very little residual sugar, making it crisp and refreshing, while Demi-Sec is much sweeter, often enjoyed as a dessert wine. The decision on sweetness level is influenced by the dosage added after disgorgement, allowing winemakers to tailor the wine to their desired style.

One of the most iconic sparkling wines is Champagne, produced exclusively in the Champagne region of France. The unique terroir of this region, with its chalky soils and cool climate, contributes to the distinctive minerality, acidity, and finesse of Champagne. The region is divided into several sub-regions, each with its own characteristics, such as the Montagne de Reims, known for its powerful Pinot Noir, and the Côte des Blancs, celebrated for its elegant Chardonnay. Champagne's reputation is built on centuries of tradition and strict regulations, ensuring that only the highest quality wines bear its name.

Beyond Champagne, many other regions produce exceptional sparkling wines. Prosecco, from Italy's Veneto region, is known for its light, fruity character and approachable price point. Made primarily from the Glera grape, Prosecco is typically produced using the Charmat Method, resulting in a fresh and aromatic wine with notes of green apple, pear, and white flowers. Prosecco's versatility makes it a popular choice for cocktails, such as the classic Bellini, as well as for casual sipping.

Cava, Spain's answer to sparkling wine, hails from the Penedès region in Catalonia. Made using the Traditional Method, Cava offers excellent value for money, often rivaling Champagne in quality at a fraction of the price. Cava is typically made from indigenous Spanish grape varieties, including Macabeo, Xarel-lo, and Parellada, which contribute to its distinctive flavor profile, characterized by citrus, apple, and almond notes. The aging process adds complexity, with Reserva and Gran Reserva Cavas offering richer, more nuanced flavors.

In addition to these well-known styles, sparkling wines are produced in many other regions around the world. The United States, particularly California, has a burgeoning sparkling wine industry, with producers crafting high-quality wines using both the Traditional and Charmat methods. The cooler climates of Oregon and Washington also produce notable sparkling wines, often made from classic Champagne grape varieties. Other countries, such as Australia, New Zealand, and South Africa, are also gaining recognition for their sparkling wines, each bringing their unique terroirs and winemaking traditions to the table.

Pairing sparkling wine with food can enhance the dining experience, thanks to its high acidity and effervescence, which cleanse the palate and complement a wide range of flavors. Brut Champagne pairs beautifully with oysters, caviar, and creamy cheeses, while its acidity cuts through rich dishes like foie gras and fried chicken. Prosecco's light, fruity profile makes it a delightful match for antipasti, sushi, and fruit-based desserts. Cava, with its versatility and balance, can be enjoyed with tapas, grilled seafood, and roasted vegetables.

Serving sparkling wine at the correct temperature is crucial to fully appreciate its nuances. Generally, sparkling wines should be served well-chilled, between 40-50°F (4-10°C). Too warm, and the wine can taste flat and overly sweet; too cold, and the flavors and aromas can be muted. Proper glassware is also important. While traditional flute glasses are popular for their aesthetic appeal, many experts suggest using white wine glasses or tulip-shaped glasses to better capture the wine's aromas and allow the bubbles to develop fully.

Dessert Wines

Dessert wines, often referred to as the sweet jewels of the viticultural world, offer a unique indulgence that can transform any meal into a memorable experience. These wines, characterized by their rich flavors and luscious sweetness, are crafted through various meticulous processes that concentrate the natural sugars in grapes. The result is a diverse array of wines, each with its own distinctive profile, capable of pairing beautifully with desserts or standing alone as a decadent treat.

The creation of dessert wines begins with the careful selection of grape varieties known for their high sugar content and aromatic potential. Commonly used grapes include Muscat, Riesling, and Chenin Blanc, but many other varieties can also produce exceptional dessert wines. The ripening process is crucial; grapes are often left on the vine longer than usual to achieve higher sugar levels, a technique known as late harvesting. This extended hang time allows the grapes to develop more complex flavors and greater sweetness.

One of the most renowned methods of producing dessert wines is the noble rot, or Botrytis cinerea, technique. This beneficial fungus selectively dehydrates the grapes, concentrating their sugars and flavors while adding unique honeyed and apricot notes. Sauternes, from the Bordeaux region of France, is perhaps the most famous example of a wine made with botrytized grapes. The vineyards of Sauternes, bathed in morning fogs and afternoon sun, create the perfect conditions for noble rot to thrive. The resulting wines boast an exquisite balance of sweetness and acidity, with layers of dried fruit, honey, and spice.

Another method involves the production of ice wine (Eiswein), which relies on natural freezing of the grapes. This technique is predominantly used in colder wine regions like Germany and Canada. Grapes are left on the vine until temperatures drop sufficiently to freeze them solid. Harvested and pressed while still frozen, the grapes yield a small amount of highly concentrated juice. Ice wines are intensely sweet with a vibrant acidity, offering flavors of ripe tropical fruits, peaches, and citrus. The labor-intensive nature of ice wine production and the limited yields contribute to its rarity and price.

In addition to noble rot and ice wines, the dried grape method, or passito, is another traditional approach to crafting dessert wines. Grapes are harvested and then dried on mats or hung in well-ventilated areas to reduce their water content and concentrate their sugars. This method is popular in regions such as Italy, where it produces wines like Vin Santo and Recioto. These wines are known for their rich, raisin-like flavors, often accompanied by notes of nuts, caramel, and dried figs.

Fortified wines, such as Port, Sherry, and Madeira, represent another important category of dessert wines. The fortification process involves adding a neutral grape spirit to the wine, which halts fermentation and preserves some of the natural sugars, resulting in a sweet, high-alcohol wine. Port, from Portugal's Douro Valley, is typically made from a blend of indigenous grape varieties and aged in oak barrels. Depending on the style—Ruby, Tawny, or Vintage—Port can exhibit a range of flavors from fresh red berries to dried fruits, nuts, and spices.

Sherry, from the Jerez region of Spain, offers a wide spectrum of styles, from dry to lusciously sweet. The sweetest Sherries, known as Pedro Ximénez (PX) and Moscatel, are made from sun-dried grapes and aged through a solera system, resulting in deeply concentrated wines with flavors of molasses, toffee, and dried fruits. Madeira, produced on the Portuguese island of the same name, is another fortified wine known for its longevity and complex flavor profile, which includes notes of caramel, nuts, and dried fruits, developed through a unique heating process called estufagem.

Pairing dessert wines with food can elevate both the wine and the dish to new heights. The key to a successful pairing is to match the wine's sweetness level with that of the dessert, ensuring that the wine does not taste overly sweet or overly dry in comparison. For example, a rich chocolate torte pairs wonderfully with a Vintage Port, whose robust flavors and tannins complement the intensity of the chocolate. A delicate lemon tart, on the other hand, finds an ideal partner in a late-harvest Riesling, whose bright acidity and citrus notes mirror the dessert's flavors.

Cheese, too, can be an excellent match for dessert wines. The salty, savory characteristics of blue cheese contrast beautifully with the sweetness of a Sauternes or a Tawny Port, creating a harmonious balance of flavors. Creamy cheeses like Brie or Camembert pair well with the nutty, caramel notes of an aged Sherry, while a sharp Cheddar can stand up to the boldness of a Madeira.

When serving dessert wines, it's important to consider the temperature. Most dessert wines are best enjoyed slightly chilled, around 50-55°F (10-13°C), which helps to balance their sweetness and enhance their aromatic complexity. Fortified wines like Port and Madeira can be served a bit warmer, around 60-65°F (15-18°C), to allow their rich flavors to fully develop. Proper glassware is also essential; smaller glasses with a narrow bowl help to concentrate the wine's aromas and prevent it from warming too quickly in the glass.

Dessert wines are not just limited to traditional pairings; they can also be used creatively in cooking. A splash of sweet Marsala can elevate a classic dish like Chicken Marsala, adding depth and richness. Poaching fruits in a dessert wine like Moscato or Sauternes can infuse them with complex flavors, creating a simple yet elegant dessert. Even a reduction of dessert wine can be drizzled over ice cream or panna cotta for a luxurious finishing touch.

For those new to dessert wines, exploring different styles and regions can be a delightful journey. Starting with a well-known wine like a Sauternes or a late-harvest Riesling provides a benchmark for sweetness and complexity. From there, branching out to try different methods and grape varieties, such as the dried grape wines of Italy or the fortified wines of Portugal and Spain, can deepen one's appreciation and understanding of this diverse category.

Fortified Wines

Fortified wines, a delightful category that combines the art of winemaking with the science of fortification, are celebrated for their robust flavors and longevity. These wines, enriched with the addition of distilled spirits, offer a unique drinking experience that spans a broad spectrum of styles, from the sweet and luscious to the dry and complex. Their origins date back centuries, with each style reflecting the traditions of its region of production.

The process of fortification involves adding a neutral grape spirit, usually brandy, to the wine either during or after fermentation. This addition increases the alcohol content and can halt fermentation, preserving some of the natural sugars of the grape, which results in a sweeter wine. Alternatively, fortification can occur after fermentation has completed, producing a dry style of fortified wine. The timing of the fortification is crucial as it defines the final character of the wine, influencing sweetness, flavor intensity, and aging potential.

Port, one of the most famous fortified wines, hails from the Douro Valley in Portugal. It is traditionally made from a blend of indigenous grape varieties, including Touriga Nacional, Tinta Roriz, and Touriga Franca. The grapes are often foot-trodden in large stone troughs called lagares, a method that has been used for centuries to extract maximum color, flavor, and tannin. After a brief fermentation period, the wine is fortified with aguardente, a neutral grape spirit, to arrest fermentation and retain natural sweetness. The fortified wine is then aged in oak barrels, where it matures and develops its characteristic depth and complexity.

There are several styles of Port, each with its own unique attributes. Ruby Port, the youngest and fruitiest style, is typically aged for a short period in large oak casks or stainless steel tanks to preserve its bright, primary fruit flavors. Tawny Port, on the other hand, is aged for longer periods in smaller barrels, allowing oxidative aging to impart nutty, caramel, and dried fruit notes. Vintage Port, made only in exceptional years, is bottled after a short period of barrel aging and can mature for decades in the bottle, evolving complex layers of flavor over time.

Sherry, from the Jerez region in Spain, offers an astonishing variety of styles, ranging from bone-dry to lusciously sweet. The production of Sherry begins with the selection of base wines, primarily from the Palomino grape. These wines are fortified and aged using the solera system, a dynamic aging process that blends wines of different ages to ensure consistency and complexity. The solera system involves a series of barrels arranged in tiers, with younger wines gradually blended with older ones as they age.

Dry Sherry styles include Fino and Manzanilla, both aged under a layer of flor yeast that protects the wine from oxidation and imparts a distinctively fresh, yeasty character. Amontillado and Oloroso Sherries, aged partially or entirely without flor, develop richer, nuttier flavors and a darker color due to exposure to oxygen. Sweet Sherries, such as Pedro Ximénez (PX) and Moscatel, are made from sun-dried grapes and aged through the solera system, resulting in intensely sweet wines with flavors of raisins, figs, and caramel.

Madeira, produced on the Portuguese island of the same name, is another remarkable fortified wine known for its resilience and longevity. The unique production process of Madeira involves heating the wine, which was historically discovered as a beneficial side effect of long sea voyages. This method, known as estufagem, involves warming the wine in special tanks or by natural heat in lofts, a process that accelerates aging and imparts distinctive flavors of caramel, dried fruit, and nuts.

Madeira wines are categorized by grape variety and sweetness level, with styles ranging from dry Sercial and Verdelho to sweet Bual and Malmsey. Each style offers a different balance of acidity and sweetness, making Madeira an exceptionally versatile wine for both drinking and cooking. Its high acidity and complex flavors allow it to pair well with a wide range of foods, from savory dishes to rich desserts.

When it comes to serving fortified wines, temperature and glassware play important roles in enhancing their enjoyment. Most fortified wines are best enjoyed slightly chilled, around 55-60°F (13-15°C), to balance their sweetness and highlight their aromatic complexity. Madeira and Tawny Port can be served a bit warmer, allowing their rich flavors to fully develop. Using smaller glasses with a narrow bowl can help concentrate the wine's aromas and prevent it from warming too quickly in the glass.

Fortified wines are incredibly versatile in culinary applications as well. A splash of dry Sherry can add depth to soups and sauces, while sweet Sherries like PX can be drizzled over vanilla ice cream or used to macerate fruits. Port, with its rich fruitiness, makes a wonderful reduction sauce for meats or can be used in decadent desserts like chocolate truffles. Madeira's robust flavors enhance everything from savory stews to rich cakes, making it a valuable addition to any kitchen.

Exploring the world of fortified wines can be a rewarding journey for both novice and experienced wine enthusiasts. Starting with well-known styles like Ruby Port or Fino Sherry provides a solid foundation, while branching out to explore the diverse range of Tawny Ports, Vintage Ports, and various Sherry and Madeira styles can deepen one's appreciation for these complex wines. Each bottle tells a story of its region, its grapes, and the meticulous craftsmanship that goes into its production.

The history and tradition behind fortified wines add an extra layer of intrigue and enjoyment. From the sun-drenched vineyards of the Douro Valley to the windswept island of Madeira, these wines reflect the unique terroirs and winemaking philosophies of their places of origin. Understanding the nuances of their production and aging processes not only enhances one's tasting experience but also fosters a greater appreciation for the dedication and skill involved in crafting each bottle.